A Note From Rick Renner

I am on a personal quest to see a "revival of the Bible" so people can establish their lives on a firm foundation that will stand strong and endure the test when the end-time storm winds begin to intensify.

In order to experience a revival of the Bible in your personal life, it is important to take time each day to read, receive, and apply its truths to your life. James tells us that if we will continue in the perfect law of liberty — refusing to be forgetful hearers but determined to be doers — we will be blessed in our ways. As you watch or listen to the programs in this series and work through this corresponding study guide, I trust that you will search the Scriptures and allow the Holy Spirit to help you hear something new from God's Word that applies specifically to your life. I encourage you to be a doer of the Word that He reveals to you. Whatever the cost, I assure you — it will be worth it.

> Thy words were found, and I did eat them;
> and thy word was unto me the joy and rejoicing of mine heart:
> for I am called by thy name, O Lord God of hosts.
> — Jeremiah 15:16

Your brother and friend in Jesus Christ,

Rick Renner

Unless otherwise indicated, all scripture quotations are taken from the *King James Version* of the Bible.

Scripture quotations marked (*MSG*) are taken from *The Message*, copyright © 1993, 2002, 2018 by Eugene H. Peterson. Used by permission of NavPress. All rights reserved. Represented by Tyndale House Publishers, Inc.

Scripture quotations marked (*NKJV*) are taken from the *New King James Version*®. Copyright © 1982 by Thomas Nelson. Used by permission. All rights reserved.

Scripture quotations marked (*NLT*) are taken from the Holy Bible, *New Living Translation*, copyright © 1996, 2004, 2015 by Tyndale House Foundation. Used by permission of Tyndale House Publishers, Inc., Carol Stream, Illinois 60188. All rights reserved.

Scripture quotations marked (*TLB*) are taken from *The Living Bible* copyright © 1971. Used by permission of Tyndale House Publishers, Inc., Carol Stream, Illinois 60188. All rights reserved.

The New Testament in Modern English by J.B. Phillips copyright © 1960, 1972 J. B. Phillips. Administered by The Archbishops' Council of the Church of England. Used by Permission.

Signs You'll See Just Before Jesus Comes

Copyright © 2020 by Rick Renner
8316 E. 73rd St.
Tulsa, Oklahoma 74133

Published by Rick Renner Ministries
www.renner.org

ISBN 13: 978-1-68031-863-0

eBook ISBN 13: 978-1-68031-864-7

All rights reserved. No portion of this book may be reproduced or transmitted in any form or by any means — electronic, mechanical, photocopy, recording, scanning, or other — except for brief quotations in critical reviews or articles, without the prior written permission of the Publisher.

How To Use This Study Guide

This ten-lesson study guide corresponds to *"Signs You'll See Just Before Jesus Comes" With Rick Renner* (Renner TV). Each lesson in this study guide covers a topic that is addressed during the program series, with questions and references supplied to draw you deeper into your own private study of the Scriptures on this subject.

To derive the most benefit from this study guide, consider the following:

First, watch or listen to the program prior to working through the corresponding lesson in this guide. (Programs can also be viewed at **renner.org** by clicking on the Media/Archives links.)

Second, take the time to look up the scriptures included in each lesson. Prayerfully consider their application to your own life.

Third, use a journal or notebook to make note of your answers to each lesson's Study Questions and Practical Application challenges.

Fourth, invest specific time in prayer and in the Word of God to consult with the Holy Spirit. Write down the scriptures or insights He reveals to you.

Finally, take action! Whatever the Lord tells you to do according to His Word, do it.

For added insights on this subject, it is recommended that you obtain Rick Renner's books *Signs You'll See Just Before Jesus Comes* and *Last Days Survival Guide: A Scriptural Handbook To Prepare You for These Perilous Times*. You may also select from Rick's other available resources by placing your order at **renner.org** or by calling 1-800-742-5593.

LESSON 1

TOPIC

Signs on a Prophetic Road

SCRIPTURES

1. **Matthew 24:1-3** — And Jesus went out, and departed from the temple: and his disciples came to him for to shew him the buildings of the temple. And Jesus said unto them, See ye not all these things? verily I say unto you, There shall not be left here one stone upon another, that shall not be thrown down. And as he sat upon the mount of Olives, the disciples came unto him privately, saying, Tell us, when shall these things be? and what shall be the sign of thy coming, and of the end of the world?

2. **Matthew 24:36** — But of that day and hour knoweth no man, no, not the angels of heaven, but my Father only.

GREEK WORDS

1. "when" — ποτέ (*pote*): specific information; seeking a concrete answer
2. "what" — τι (*ti*): minute, minuscule detail; exactly; explicitly
3. "sign" — σημεῖον (*semeion*): a marker or sign to alert a traveler to where he is on a road; authenticating marks, or specific signs
4. "end" — συντέλειας (*sunteleias*): the closure, summation, or wrap-up of the age
5. "world" — αἰῶνος (*aionos*): not the world itself, but age

SYNOPSIS

The ten lessons in this study on ***Signs You'll See Just Before Jesus Comes*** will focus on the following topics:

- Signs on a Prophetic Road
- Where Are We in Time?
- Worldwide Deception
- Wars, Commotions, Nations and Kingdoms Against Nations and Kingdoms

- Famine, Scarcity, Economic Woes, Pestilence, and Diseases
- Catastrophic Events, Monstrous Developments, Signs From the Heavens
- Worldwide Persecution
- The Emergence of False Prophets
- The Love of Many Will Wax Cold
- The Ultimate Sign That Jesus Is Coming Soon

The emphasis of this lesson:

Matthew 24 captures a conversation between Jesus and His disciples in which He reveals specific prophetic signs we will see before He comes and before the end of the age. This same conversation is also recorded in the gospels of Mark and Luke and includes additional details.

One day as Jesus and His disciples were leaving the temple, "…He told them, 'All these buildings will be knocked down, with not one stone left on top of another!'" (Matthew 24:2 *TLB*) Clearly, the disciples were stunned by Jesus' words, and they pressed Him privately to know what the signs would be that would precede such an unthinkable event. Jesus then began to unpack in detail numerous signs we would see before His coming and before the end of the age.

What is interesting is that if you travel to the city of Jerusalem today, you will see a massive mound of huge stones just adjacent to the western wall. These stones were actually once a part of the temple during Jesus' day. About 40 years after Jesus prophesied that the temple would be torn down, Emperor Titus and the Roman army invaded Jerusalem and did just what Jesus said. The massive pile of stones is a tangible sign of the fulfillment of Jesus's words. In fact, they are a guarantee that everything that Jesus spoke in Matthew 24 will also come to pass.

A Candid Conversation Between Jesus and His Disciples

There is a very interesting conversation between Jesus and His disciples recorded in Matthew's gospel. The Bible says, "And Jesus went out, and departed from the temple: and his disciples came to him for to shew him the buildings of the temple" (Matthew 24:1). This temple was the one erected by Herod the Great, and while it was not as glorious as the original temple built by King Solomon, it was magnificent nonetheless and occupied an area of one stadium according to the historian Josephus.

The Bible goes on to say, "And Jesus said unto them, See ye not all these things? verily I say unto you, There shall not be left here one stone upon another, that shall not be thrown down" (Matthew 24:2). No sooner had these words left Jesus' lips that the questions in the minds of the disciples began to swirl. They thought: *How can this be? These stones are simply massive and weigh tons. How in the world will they be thrown down and scattered?*

Greatly perplexed by Jesus' words, the disciples looked for an opportunity to ask Him about what He said. The Bible says, "And as he sat upon the mount of Olives, the disciples came unto him privately, saying, Tell us, when shall these things be? and what shall be the sign of thy coming, and of the end of the world?" (Matthew 24:3) In this verse, there are five very important words that we need to understand. Let's take a closer look at: "when," "what," "sign," "end," and "world."

'When shall these things be?'

The first question the disciples asked Jesus is, "*When* shall these things be?" The word "when" is the Greek word *pote*, and it describes *specific information*. It signifies *one seeking a concrete answer*. The disciples were questioning Jesus and asking for *specific information* regarding the timing of the destruction of the temple, the sign of His coming, and the sign indicating the end of the world. They felt the liberty to ask the Lord for very specific, concrete information, and so should you.

'What shall be the sign of thy coming?'

The second question the disciples posed to Jesus was, "*What* shall be the sign of thy coming?" The word "what" here is the little Greek word *ti*, which describes *the most minute, minuscule detail*. The disciples were asking Jesus *exactly* and *explicitly* what the sign of His coming would be. The use of this word is the equivalent of them saying, "Lord, tell us *explicitly* and *exactly* — down to the *minutest detail* — what will be the sign of your coming."

The Disciples Wanted To Know the 'Sign'

Jesus' most devoted followers asked Him for the "sign" of His coming. The word "sign" in Matthew 24:3 is the Greek word *semeion*, and it describes *a marker or sign to alert a traveler to where he is on a road*. This word denotes *authenticating marks*, or *specific signs* that tell a person where he is.

Imagine you're planning a vacation to the Great Smoky Mountains in Tennessee. You chart your course and set out on your journey. Once you get on the highway and begin heading in the direction of eastern Tennessee, you begin to see signs showing how far you are from your destination. Each sign lets you know exactly where you are on your journey. Then the closer you get to the Smoky Mountains, the more signs you see letting you know you're approaching your destination. As soon as you arrive at the entrance to the national park, you're greeted by a massive sign confirming that you have finally reached your journey's end. You're no longer *approaching* the territory of your destination — you have *arrived*! That is the idea communicated in the Greek word *semeion* — translated here as "sign."

The disciples were asking Jesus for a very specific "sign" of His coming. They wanted to know the *authenticating mark* or *markers* that would alert them to where they were on the prophetic road to the end of the world.

The 'End of the World'

In addition to wanting to know when the temple would be destroyed and when Jesus would return, the disciples also wanted to know the sign "…of the end of the world" (Matthew 24:3). The Greek word for "end" here is the word *sunteleias*, which describes *the closure, summation, or wrap-up of something*. And the word "world" is the Greek word *aionos*, which does not describe the world, the earth, or the universe. The word *aionos* means *the age*.

Therefore, a better translation of this portion of the verse would be, "How will we know that we're approaching the closure or the wrap-up of the age?"

Jesus Provided a Detailed List of Signs

With a willingness to provide answers to the disciples' questions, Jesus began to download concrete information and give a detailed list of specific signs that they would see on their journey toward the wrap-up or consummation of all things. These are actually listed in three of the four gospels: **Matthew 24:4-14; Mark 13:5-13; Luke 21:8-19.**

1. Worldwide deception (Matthew 24:4)
2. Deception in the Church (Matthew 24:5)
3. Wars (Matthew 24:6)
4. Rumors of wars (Matthew 24:6)
5. Commotions (Luke 21:9)
6. Widespread terrorism (Luke 21:9)
7. Warring political systems (Matthew 24:7)
8. Clash of culture (Matthew 24:7)
9. Ethnic conflicts (Matthew 24:7)
10. Famines (Matthew 24:7)
11. Economic instability (Matthew 24:7)
12. Pestilences (Matthew 24:7)
13. Emergence of unknown diseases (Matthew 24:7)
14. Great seismic activity (Matthew 24:7)
15. Widespread persecution (Matthew 24:9)
16. Legal prosecution of Christians (Matthew 24:9)
17. Imprisonment of believers (Matthew 24:9)
18. Emergence of false prophets (Matthew 24:11)
19. Love of many waxing cold (Matthew 24:12)
20. Fearful sights (Luke 21:11)
21. Signs from the heavens (Luke 21:11)
22. Worldwide preaching of the Gospel (Matthew 24:14)

Jesus named all of these specific signs we would see before His return and before the end of the age. In reality, we have seen many of these signs taking place for years — in some cases, thousands of years. However, Jesus said that as we come to the "end of the world" — the *closure* or *wrap-up* (*sunteleias*) of the *age* (*aionos*) — these signs will increase in number, in frequency, and in intensity.

Now it is imperative to realize that Jesus did not tell us these things to scare us. He told us these things to *prepare* us. He loves us dearly and wants us to be ready for what is coming in the future. This is especially true for those of us who are living in the last of the last days. The fact of the matter is we are seeing in our day what the apostle Paul and countless others prophesied years ago would take place. They saw these things from a distance, but we are seeing them in real-time.

Jesus went on to say, "But of that day and hour knoweth no man, no, not the angels of heaven, but my Father only" (Matthew 24:36). Although we cannot know the *specific day* or the *specific hour* that Jesus will return, we can certainly know the season. That is why He gave His disciples — which includes us — this list of specific signs. He said, "…When ye shall see all these things, know that it is near, even at the doors" (Matthew 24:33).

In our next lesson, we will take a closer look at where we are in time in light of our current events and all the signs Jesus prophesied would take place.

STUDY QUESTIONS

> **Study to shew thyself approved unto God, a workman that needeth not to be ashamed, rightly dividing the word of truth.**
> — 2 Timothy 2:15

1. Without question, we are living in unprecedented times. There are things happening all around us that are unlike anything we've ever seen. From your perspective, what are some of the most bizarre things you see taking place in the world around you?
2. In three of the four gospels, Jesus gives us more than 20 specific signs regarding His return to earth and the end of the age. Which of these end-time markers can you actually see taking place right now near you and around the world?

PRACTICAL APPLICATION

> But be ye doers of the word, and not hearers only, deceiving your own selves.
> — James 1:22

1. When the disciples came to Jesus on the Mount of Olives, they asked Him for very *specific, concrete* information. When you seek the Lord in prayer, do you ask Him for very specific things? Or are your requests broad, general, and non-specific? How do you think praying for specific things can potentially energize your faith?

2. What specific, concrete wisdom or direction do you need right now? Take a few moments to pray and ask the Holy Spirit to tell you what you need to know in order to make the best decisions for you and your family. (Reflect and stand on God's promises to you in Psalm 32:8; Jeremiah 29:11; and James 1:5.)

LESSON 2

TOPIC

Where Are We in Time?

SCRIPTURES

1. **Matthew 24:1-3** — And Jesus went out, and departed from the temple: and his disciples came to him for to shew him the buildings of the temple. And Jesus said unto them, See ye not all these things? verily I say unto you, There shall not be left here one stone upon another, that shall not be thrown down. And as he sat upon the mount of Olives, the disciples came unto him privately, saying, Tell us, when shall these things be? and what shall be the sign of thy coming, and of the end of the world?
2. **Matthew 24:3 (*NKJV*)** — ...What will be the sign of Your coming, and of the end of the age?
3. **Matthew 24:8** — All these are the beginning of sorrows.
4. **Matthew 24:36** — But of that day and hour knoweth no man, no, not the angels of heaven, but my Father only.
5. **John 16:13** — Howbeit when he, the Spirit of truth, is come, he will guide you into all truth: for he shall not speak of himself; but whatsoever he shall hear, that shall he speak: and he will shew you things to come.
6. **2 Peter 3:3,4 (*NLT*)** — ...In the last days scoffers will come, mocking the truth and following their own desires. They will say, 'What happened to the promise that Jesus is coming again?
7. **2 Timothy 1:7** — For God hath not given us the spirit of fear; but of power, and of love, and of a sound mind
8. **Romans 8:37** — ...in all these things we are more than conquerors through him that loved us.

GREEK WORDS
1. "when" — ποτέ (*pote*): specific information; seeking a concrete answer
2. "what" — τι (*ti*): minute, minuscule detail; exactly; explicitly
3. "sign" — σημεῖον (*semeion*): a marker or sign to alert a traveler to where he is on a road; authenticating marks, or specific signs
4. "end" — συντέλειας (*sunteleias*): the closure, summation, or wrap-up of the age
5. "world" — αἰῶνος (*aionos*): not the world itself, but age
6. "sorrows" — ὠδίν (*oodin*): birth pains; pain of childbirth; contractions; the pain necessary to open up or to introduce something new
7. "guide" — ὁδηγός (*hodegos*): guide; road guide; one who leads you on an excursion
8. "show" — ἀναγγέλλω (*anangello*): to declare; to make clear; to clearly and vividly portray; to rehearse
9. "things to come" — τὰ ἐρχόμενα (*ta erchomena*): the things coming
10. "more than conquerors" — ὑπερνικάω (*hupernikao*): compound of the Greek words ὑπέρ (*huper*) and νικάω (*nikao*); the word (*huper*) in this case means over, above, and beyond, and it carries the idea of superiority — something that is utmost, paramount, foremost, first-rate, first-class, top-notch; greater, higher, better than, superior to, unsurpassed, unequaled, and unrivaled by any person or thing; the word νικάω (*nikao*) depicts an overcomer, a conqueror, a champion, a victor, or a master; compounded, it describes an unrivaled overcomer, an unsurpassed conqueror, or a paramount victor — a walloping, conquering force

SYNOPSIS
In the year 70 AD, Emperor Titus invaded the city of Jerusalem and gave orders to the Roman troops to utterly destroy the Jewish temple. What had taken King Herod decades to renovate and build was quickly demolished by enemy invaders. Today, more than 2,000 years later, there stands a huge pile of massive stones that once made up the magnificent temple. They are a vivid reminder of the fulfillment of Jesus' words in Matthew 24.

The Bible says, "Jesus then left the Temple. As he walked away, his disciples pointed out how very impressive the Temple architecture was. Jesus said, 'You're not impressed by all this sheer size, are you? The truth of the matter is that there's not a stone in that building that is not going to end up in a pile of rubble" (Matthew 24:1,2 *MSG*).

What Jesus prophesied is exactly what took place. But that was not all He told the disciples. Matthew's gospel documents, in great detail, a list of things that Jesus said would transpire in the future before His return and before the end of the age. As believers who are living in the last days, we need to hear Jesus' words and understand the signs that we'll see before He comes again. He gave us these prophetic markers not to scare us, but to prepare us to live victoriously in this volatile time.

The emphasis of this lesson:

Jesus prophesied that the closer we get to the end of the age, the greater the frequency and intensity of the *pains* society will be experiencing. An increase in catastrophic events is a major indication that the end of the age is near. These signs will continue to take place all the way up to the rapture of the Church. The Great Tribulation will immediately follow.

Jesus Answered the Disciples' Questions

As we saw in our first lesson, Matthew records a unique Q&A session between Jesus and His disciples as they were leaving the temple. The Bible says, "And Jesus went out, and departed from the temple: and his disciples came to him for to shew him the buildings of the temple" (Matthew 24:1). This temple, which had been totally renovated and expanded by Herod the Great, was quite remarkable, and that is what the disciples were pointing out to Jesus.

The Bible goes on to say, "And Jesus said unto them, See ye not all these things? verily I say unto you, There shall not be left here one stone upon another, that shall not be thrown down" (Matthew 24:2). These prophetic words — that not one stone of the temple would be left upon another — were fulfilled about 40 years later when Rome invaded Jerusalem in 70 AD and totally decimated the temple.

Without question, Jesus' words were quite alarming to the disciples, which is why they pressed Him for answers as soon as they got Him alone. Matthew 24:3 says, "And as he [Jesus] sat upon the mount of Olives, the disciples came unto him privately, saying, Tell us, when shall these things be? and what shall be the sign of thy coming, and of the end of the world?" Notice what the disciples were asking in this verse:

First: 'When Shall These Things Be?'

The word "when" here is the Greek word *pote*, and it describes *specific information* or *a concrete answer*. The disciples were asking Jesus for *specific, concrete information* regarding "when" the temple would be destroyed, "when" He was coming back, and "when" the end of the world would be. They felt the liberty to ask the Lord for very specific, concrete information, and so should you.

Second: 'What Shall Be the Sign of Thy Coming?'

The second question the disciples asked Jesus was, "*What* shall be the sign of thy coming?" The word "what" here is a translation of the Greek word *ti*, which describes *the most minute, minuscule detail*. The use of this word lets us know that the disciples were saying, "Lord, don't be vague and leave us in the dark. Please tell us *exactly* and *explicitly* what the sign of Your coming will be."

Third: 'Give Us the Sign'

The Greek word for "sign" in Matthew 24:3 is the word *semeion*, and it describes *a marker or sign to alert a traveler to where he is on a road*. It is an *authenticating mark*, or *specific sign* that tells a person where he is. Think about what it would be like if you were traveling down the road, and there were no signs to tell you where you were. Without signs telling you where you were, you would pass by your destination and end up wandering around aimlessly.

Signs confirm where you are and that you have arrived at your destination. That is what the word *semeion* — translated here as "sign" — means. The disciples were asking Jesus for a very specific *authenticating mark* or *markers* that would alert them to where they were on the prophetic timeline of history.

Fourth: When Is the 'End of the World'?

The Bible says that the disciples wanted to know the sign "…of the end of the world" (Matthew 24:3). The word "end" here is the Greek word *sunteleias*, which describes *the closure, summation, or wrap-up of something*. And the word "world" is the Greek word *aionos*, which does not describe the world, the earth, or the universe. The word *aionos* describes *an age*.

Actually, the *New King James Version* of Matthew 24:3 translates it like this: "...What will be the sign of Your coming, and of the end of the age?"

Essentially, the disciples were asking Jesus, "Lord, please tell us what signs we're going to see along the prophetic road to the end of the age to let us know where we are and how much further we have to go."

Three Gospels Record the Signs Jesus Gave

The Bible has a great deal to say about the end times and the return of Christ, and this particular discourse between Jesus and His disciples on the Mount of Olives which is recorded in three of the four gospels — Matthew 24:4-14; Mark 13:5-13; and Luke 21:8-19. What are the signs that we will see on our way to the wrap-up of the age?

1. Worldwide deception (Matthew 24:4)
2. Deception in the Church (Matthew 24:5)
3. Wars (Matthew 24:6)
4. Rumors of wars (Matthew 24:6)
5. Commotions (Luke 21:9)
6. Widespread terrorism (Luke 21:9)
7. Warring political systems (Matthew 24:7)
8. Clash of culture (Matthew 24:7)
9. Ethnic conflicts (Matthew 24:7)
10. Famines (Matthew 24:7)
11. Economic instability (Matthew 24:7)
12. Pestilences (Matthew 24:7)
13. Emergence of unknown diseases (Matthew 24:7)
14. Great seismic activity (Matthew 24:7)
15. Widespread persecution (Matthew 24:9)
16. Legal prosecution of Christians (Matthew 24:9)
17. Imprisonment of believers (Matthew 24:9)
18. Emergence of false prophets (Matthew 24:11)
19. Love of many waxing cold (Matthew 24:12)
20. Fearful sights (Luke 21:11)
21. Signs from the heavens (Luke 21:11)
22. Worldwide preaching of the Gospel (Matthew 24:14)

All of these are signs that Jesus Himself said the inhabitants of the earth would see as we come to the end of the age. The closer and closer we get to the end, the more frequent, the more numerous, and the more intense these signs will become.

These Signs Are the Beginning of 'Sorrows'

As Jesus was giving this list of signs, He injected, "All these are the beginning of sorrows" (Matthew 24:8). The word "sorrows" here is the Greek word *oodin*, which describes *birth pains* or *the pain of childbirth*. It specifically denotes the *contractions* a woman experiences before she gives birth to her child. Furthermore, this word *oodin* — translated here as "sorrows" — can also describe *the pain necessary to open up or to introduce something new.*

Stop and think about a woman who is about to give birth. At the very beginning of her labor, her contractions are sporadic and spaced out. But as she comes closer and closer to the time of delivery, her contractions increase in number and in intensity. Eventually, they become so frequent and severe that she can no longer discern when one ends and the next one begins. This is her body's way of opening up to bring her new baby into the world.

By using this word "sorrows" — the Greek word *oodin* — Jesus is telling us that before His return and the wrap-up of this age, the world and its inhabitants will begin to experience contraction-like pains. The closer and closer we get to the very end, the greater the frequency and intensity of the pains society will be experiencing — just like a woman getting ready to give birth to a child. And once those contractions start, they cannot be stopped.

A careful look at the last hundred years reveals that there have been sporadic cataclysmic events taking place all over the world. This includes political upheavals, changes in the Earth's atmosphere and physical structure, and unthinkable happenings in society at large. But if we look at the last 25 years — or just the last 10 years — we can see a dramatic increase in the frequency and intensity of catastrophic occurrences. It seems as though things that used to be rare are now happening one after another after another. Jesus prophesied this would be a major indication that the very end of the age is near. Thus, disastrous events are going to continue occurring more and more and get closer and closer all the way up to His return. In fact, they will become so numerous it will be hard to tell when one ends and the next one begins.

Regarding the time of His return, Jesus said, "But of that day and hour knoweth no man, no, not the angels of heaven, but my Father only" (Matthew 24:36). If anyone ever gives you an exact date when Jesus is coming back, don't listen to them. They don't know what they're talking about. Jesus said no one knows the exact day and hour.

Nevertheless, while we cannot know the specific *day* and *hour* that He will return, we can certainly know the season. That is why Jesus gave us the detailed list of specific signs. He said, "…When ye shall see all these things, know that it is near, even at the doors" (Matthew 24:33).

The Holy Spirit Is Our 'Guide'

Next to Jesus, the greatest gift God has given us is the gift of His Holy Spirit. In John 16:13, Jesus said, "Howbeit when he, the Spirit of truth, is come, he will guide you into all truth: for he shall not speak of himself; but whatsoever he shall hear, that shall he speak: and he will shew you things to come."

Notice the word "guide" in this verse. It is the Greek word *hodegos*, which is the word for *a guide*. Specifically, it denotes *a road guide* or *one who leads you on an excursion*. If you have ever been on a tour, you have likely had a tour guide, and that tour guide is the one who knows all the best routes to take to see all the best sights. They also know which places to avoid.

Jesus said that the Holy Spirit is given to you as a *guide*, and if you will stay in relationship with Him and listen to what He says, He will show you what roads to take and what roads to avoid. He is the Spirit of truth who is guiding you into all truth. In fact, Jesus said the Spirit will "…show you things to come" (John 16:13).

The word "show" here is the Greek word *anangello*, which means *to declare*, *to make clear*, or *to clearly and vividly portray*. Interestingly, this word also means *to rehearse*. So in addition to the Holy Spirit *declaring* and *making things vividly clear* for you, He will also *rehearse* things that are coming in the future. He will say it again and again and again until you fully comprehend it. As your all-knowing Guide, He will direct your steps and lead you down the best path possible to fulfill the call of God on your life.

Where Does the Rapture Fit Into All This?

Now you may be thinking, *What about the rapture of the Church? Where does it fit into all of this?* Those are good questions. The apostle Paul gives us a snapshot of the rapture in First Thessalonians 4:15-17: "For this we say unto you by the word of the Lord, that we which are alive and remain unto the coming of the Lord shall not prevent them which are asleep. For the Lord himself shall descend from heaven with a shout, with the voice of the archangel, and with the trump of God: and the dead in Christ shall rise first: Then we which are alive and remain shall be caught up together with them in the clouds, to meet the Lord in the air: and so shall we ever be with the Lord."

Once all the believers in Christ — those who have died and those who are still alive on earth — have been suddenly snatched out of the earth to meet Jesus in the air, the Great Tribulation will begin. The Tribulation will be a time of darkness and great agony like the world has never known. The Antichrist will suddenly be revealed and rise to power, creating a one-world government that is totally under his control. At the same time, God will begin pouring out His wrath upon all the inhabitants of the earth who rejected Him and the free gift of His Son Jesus.

All the authenticating signs that Jesus mentioned in Scripture will be taking place right up to the time of the rapture of the Church. In that split second of time, the Church Age will end and the next age will begin, which is the Great Tribulation. At the very end of the Tribulation, Jesus will return with all the saints to set up His millennial kingdom (*see* Jude 14).

We Are Living in the Last Days

Now, you may have heard people scoff and say, "Oh, they've been saying it's 'the last days' for 2,000 years." If you've heard people make that statement, you've been a firsthand witness to the fulfillment of prophecy. The apostle Peter predicted this would happen. He said, "...In the last days scoffers will come, mocking the truth and following their own desires. They will say, 'What happened to the promise that Jesus is coming again?'" (2 Peter 3:3,4 *NLT*).

The fact of the matter is, we *have* been in the last days for 2,000 years! Peter actually confirmed this on the Day of Pentecost when he stood up and preached to the people who were gathered in Jerusalem (*see* Acts

2:16-18). The day the Holy Spirit was poured out on the believers in the Upper Room was the beginning of the last days. Hence, we have prophetically been living in the last days for more than 2,000 years.

The signs that Jesus gave in the gospels are happening all around us. The end-time clock is ticking, and we are rapidly racing toward the end of the age. Again, Jesus didn't tell us these things to scare us, but to prepare us and help us know how to live in these last of the last days. The Bible says, "For God hath not given us the spirit of fear; but of power, and of love, and of a sound mind" (2 Timothy 1:7).

It's true that there will be difficulties we will face, but through the empowerment of the Holy Spirit, "...In all these things we are more than conquerors through him that loved us" (Romans 8:37). The phrase "more than conquerors" is a translation of the Greek word *hupernikao*. It is a compound of the Greek words *huper* and *nikao*. The word *huper* in this case means *over, above, and beyond*, and it carries the idea of *superiority* — something that is *utmost, paramount, foremost, first-rate, first-class, top-notch; greater, higher, better than, superior to, unsurpassed, unequaled, and unrivaled by any person or thing*. The word *nikao* depicts *an overcomer, a conqueror, a champion, a victor*, or *a master*. When these words are compounded to form the new word *hupernikao*, it describes *an unrivaled overcomer, an unsurpassed conqueror, or a paramount victor — a walloping, conquering force*.

Friend, that is what you are — *a walloping, conquering force*! In our next lesson, we will examine the number one sign Jesus said we would see before His return and the end of the age — worldwide deception.

STUDY QUESTIONS

Study to shew thyself approved unto God, a workman that needeth not to be ashamed, rightly dividing the word of truth.
— 2 Timothy 2:15

1. The New Testament has much to say about the ministry of the Holy Spirit. Check out these passages from Scripture and identify some of the ways He is available to help you.
   - Romans 8:14-16; Galatians 4:6; and 1 John 3:24
   - John 15:26 and 16:13-15
   - John 14:26; 1 Corinthians 2:13; and 1 John 2:27

- John 6:63; Romans 8:11; and 2 Corinthians 3:6
- Acts 1:8

2. According to Second Peter 3:3-6, what will scoffers in the last days willfully ignore? Where are you seeing this take place? In what other ways are you seeing people mock and jeer at the truth of God's Word?

PRACTICAL APPLICATION

> But be ye doers of the word, and not hearers only, deceiving your own selves.
> —James 1:22

1. In what ways has the culture changed from when you were growing up? How has the world rapidly departed from time-tested beliefs and traditions that are based on biblical, Judeo-Christian values?

2. Jesus said that the Holy Spirit has been given to you to *teach you all things* and *guide you into all truth*. Stop and think: What are a few of the amazing things that the Holy Spirit has taught you since you entered into relationship with Jesus? What truths about God's character and His Word has the Spirit made real to you? What truths about yourself has He opened your eyes to?

LESSON 3

TOPIC

Worldwide Deception

SCRIPTURES

1. **Matthew 24:3-5** — And as he sat upon the mount of Olives, the disciples came unto him privately, saying, Tell us, when shall these things be? and what shall be the sign of thy coming, and of the end of the world? And Jesus answered and said unto them, Take heed that no man deceive you. For many shall come in my name, saying, I am Christ; and shall deceive many.

2. **2 Thessalonians 2:3** — Let no man deceive you by any means: for that day shall not come, except there come a falling away first, and that man of sin be revealed, the son of perdition.
3. **2 Thessalonians 2:11** — And for this cause God shall send them strong delusion, that they should believe a lie.
4. **1 Timothy 4:1** — Now the Spirit speaketh expressly, that in the latter times some shall depart from the faith, giving heed to seducing spirits, and doctrines of devils.

GREEK WORDS

1. "when" — ποτέ (*pote*): specific information; seeking a concrete answer
2. "what" — τι (*ti*): minute, minuscule detail; exactly; explicitly
3. "sign" — σημεῖον (*semeion*): a marker or sign to alert a traveler to where he is on a road; authenticating marks, or specific signs
4. "end" — συντέλειας (*sunteleias*): the closure, summation, or wrap-up of the age
5. "world" — αἰῶνος (*aionos*): not the world itself, but age
6. "take heed" — βλέπω (*blepo*): watch; pay attention; intended to jar and jolt his listeners
7. "deceive" — πλανάω (*planao*): a deceptive, moral wandering; pictures a people who have veered from a solid path; those who teeter on a dangerous moral path; to morally falter
8. "falling away" — ἀποστασία (*apostasia*): a falling away or revolt; describes political revolt
9. "first" — πρῶτον (*proton*): first in order; in first-place; to begin with
10. "and for this cause" — καὶ διὰ τοῦτο (*kai dia touto*): for this reason; because of this; pictures God's response to their choice
11. "send" — πέμπω (*pempo*): to send; a willful sending or dispatching
12. "strong delusion" — ἐνέργειαν πλάνης (*energeian planes*): the word ἐνεργέω (*energeo*) and πλάνη (*plane*); the word ἐνεργέω (*energeo*) depicts a force propelling something forward or an energy that ignites a process and facilitates it all the way to its conclusion; the word πλάνη (*plane*) pictures wandering, or deviant behavior; to leave a solid moral path; used to depict an animal that lost its way and could never find its way back home

13. "in my name" — ἐπὶ τῷ ὀνόματί μου (*epi to onomati mou*): on the reputation or strength of my name
14. "saying" — λέγοντες (*legontes*): alleging; claiming; purporting
15. "Christ" — χριστός (*christos*): the Greek word for the anointing
16. "deceive" — πλανάω (*planao*): pictures delusion; a moral wandering; a moral wandering from the foundational doctrines of the Bible, resulting in confusion about what is right or wrong; a delusion that will work in society at the end of the age
17. "expressly" — ῥητῶς (*rhetos*): explicitly; undeniable, unmistakable terms
18. "latter" — ὕστερον (*husteron*): at the very end; at the final conclusion
19. "shall depart" — ἀφίστημι (*apistemi*): to change positions; a slow, methodical departure

SYNOPSIS

Located in the ancient city of Hierapolis is a place called the *bouleuterion*. The word "bouleuterion" comes from the Greek word *boule*, which means *to counsel*. Hence, the *bouleuterion* was literally *the place of the counselors*. History reveals that during the First Century, virtually every ancient Greek and Roman city had a *bouleuterion* where the city counselors met regularly to discuss all the issues of the city. They talked about taxes, laws, marriage issues, alcohol addiction, and problems plaguing society.

Make no mistake: the First Century was a very dark time filled with many challenges, and the city counselors were always looking for answers to the problems people were facing. Yet, it was nothing to be compared with what will take place in society at the end of the age. In First Timothy 4:1, the apostle Paul said, "Now the Spirit speaketh expressly, that in the latter times some shall depart from the faith, giving heed to seducing spirits, and doctrines of devils."

Under the inspiration of the Holy Spirit, Paul gives this emphatic warning that in the last of the last days, a sizable cross-section of people in the Church are going to withdraw from their long-held faith in God, and it will be the result of increased demonic activity running rampant in the world. Thankfully, we don't have to become a statistic in this falling away. We have the Holy Spirit as our guide, teaching us how to live victoriously in the midst of difficult times.

The emphasis of this lesson:

The first sign that Jesus gave indicating that we are nearing the end of the age is worldwide deception. This widespread departure from the truth will also infiltrate the Church, causing a number of believers to gradually withdraw and fall away from faith in Jesus Christ.

A Review of Our Anchor Verse

In Matthew 24, Jesus and His disciples were leaving the temple area in Jerusalem traveling east, and in verse 3 the Bible says, "And as he [Jesus] sat upon the mount of Olives, the disciples came unto him privately, saying, Tell us, when shall these things be? and what shall be the sign of thy coming, and of the end of the world?" There are five important words in this verse that we really need to understand.

The first word is the word "when." The disciples asked, "*When* shall these things be?" The word "when" is the Greek word *pote*, and it describes *specific information* and pictures *one seeking a concrete answer*. The disciples asked for very specific, concrete information regarding when the things that Jesus had said would take place.

The second word is the word "what." The disciples asked, "What shall be the sign of thy coming?" In Greek, the word "what" is the word *ti*, which describes *a minute, minuscule detail*. The use of this word lets us know that the disciples were saying, "Lord, don't be vague. Tell us *exactly* and *explicitly* — down to the tiniest detail — what the sign of Your coming will be."

The third important word is the word "sign." In Greek, "sign" is the word *semeion*, and it describes *a marker or sign to alert a traveler to where he is on a road*. "Signs" are *authenticating marks, or specific signs* letting one know how much further he has to go to reach his destination. If we don't have signs, we roam aimlessly, not knowing where we are. The use of this word is the equivalent of the disciples saying, "Lord, please reveal to us the authenticating markers we will see on the road to the end of the world. What are the *signs* that will alert us to how much more we have to go before You return?"

The fourth word to take note of is "end." The word "end" is the Greek word *sunteleias*, and it describes *the closure, summation, or wrap-up of something*. The inclusion of this word lets us know that the disciples had an inner knowing that eventually everything would run its course and come to an end. When the present age ends, it will give birth to a new age, which the Bible calls the Great Tribulation.

The fifth important word is the word "world." It is the Greek word *aionos*, which does not describe the world, the earth, or the universe. The word *aionos* describes *an age*. Every age has a concrete beginning and a concrete end, and the disciples were asking Jesus to tell them explicitly and exactly what the authenticating sign of His coming would be and when they had reached the end of the age.

Worldwide Deception Is the First Sign Jesus Gave

What was Jesus' response to the disciples' questions? The Bible says, "And Jesus answered and said unto them, Take heed that no man deceive you" (Matthew 24:4). The first sign we can expect to see before Jesus comes and this present age wraps up is worldwide deception.

The phrase "take heed" is a form of the Greek word *blepo*, which in this verse means *watch* or *pay attention*. It is spoken in such a strong tense it was intended to jar and jolt the listeners. It is as if Jesus was saying, "Stand up, throw your shoulders back, open your ears, watch, listen, be attentive, and really pay attention."

Once Jesus had acquired the disciples' full attention, He unveiled the first and foremost sign that will mark the end of the age saying, "...Take heed that no man deceive you" (Mathew 24:4). The word "deceive" here is a translation of the Greek word *planao*, which depicts *a deceptive, moral wandering*; it pictures *a people who have veered from a solid path*.

The word "deceive" used in Matthew 24:4 can also mean *to wonder off course*. It can depict *an individual who has wondered off course* or even describes *a whole nation or even vast numbers of nations that have veered off course from a moral position they once held to be true*. It suggests *a moral wondering on a worldwide scale* at the close of the age.

In Greek, this word "deceive" depicts the behavior of someone who once walked on a solid path but who is now drifting and teetering on the edge of a treacherous route. This person has either already departed from his once solid path and has lost his bearings as a result, or he is in the process of departing from it. This word "deceive" means he is going cross grain against all that was once a part of his core belief system and sadly, he is now deviating from his former solid moral position to a course that is unreliable, unpredictable and even dangerous. This word "deceive" tells us emphatically that there will be a mass divergence from time-tested biblical standards at the very end of the age.

By using the word *planao* — translated as "deceive" in Matthew 24:4 — Jesus was foretelling that a moment was coming when society would move away from the long-affirmed laws of Scripture. Although He specified many signs to indicate the conclusion of the age, He declared this mass divergence from truth — a worldwide moral wondering — would be the first, foremost and primary sign to alert us that the end was near.

The words of Matthew 24:4 are intended to let us know that those who live at the very end of the age will see moral confusion in society as deception attempts to engulf humanity with misinformation about what is morally right and wrong. It is simply a fact that we are watching this moral confusion rage across the world as never before in our lifetime.

The confusion is perhaps no clearer anywhere than the debate over gender identity — a manifestation of confusion so severe that it stuns most thinking people. The culture most of us knew when we were growing up in was Judeo Christian. But now as the winds of change are blowing, we're watching as the world is rapidly departing from time-tested beliefs and traditions that are based on biblical values. And as a result of this near abandonment of truth and throwing away of moral foundations, confusion abounds in society that is teetering on a treacherous path. All of this meaning is packed in the word "deceive" in Matthew 24:4.

A 'Falling Away' Must Take Place First Before Jesus Returns for the Church

The apostle Paul addressed the crisis of worldwide deception in Second Thessalonians 2:3 by issuing this warning: "Let no man deceive you by any means: for that day shall not come, except there come a falling away first, and that man of sin be revealed, the son of perdition."

First of all, when Paul talks about "that day," he is referring to the return of Christ. Thus, he says that the rapture of the Church will not take place until there is a "falling away first." In Greek, the word "first" is *proton*, and it means *first in order*, *in first-place*; or *to begin with*.

The Greek word for "falling away" is a translation of the word *apostasia*, which is where we get the word *apostasy*. It is a compound of the word *apo*, which means *away*, and the word *stasia*, which means *to step*. When these words are compounded to form *apostasia*, it describes *a falling away or revolt*. It is even the word for a *mutiny*.

Immediately on the heels of the great apostasy and Jesus coming back to gather the Church to Himself, the Bible says, "...that man of sin [will] be revealed, the son of perdition" (2 Thessalonians 2:3). The Greek word for "sin" here means *lawlessness*. So *the man of lawlessness* will suddenly be unveiled once the Church is taken out of the way.

The world will never embrace the man of lawlessness until the world becomes lawless itself. "Lawless" means *without God's principles* or *departing from God's standards*. In that dense, dark season of time, people will throw themselves open to every conceivable new idea and totally depart from the time-tested, solid path of Scripture. They will teeter on the edge of something very dangerous morally and will become so open-minded they will receive the man of lawlessness whom the Bible calls the Anti-Christ.

God Will Send Unbelievers 'Strong Delusion'

Paul went on to say in Second Thessalonians 2:11, "And for this cause God shall send them strong delusion, that they should believe a lie." In Greek, the phrase "and for this cause" is *kai dia touto*, which means *for this reason* or *because of this*. It pictures God's response to the world that has rejected Him. To those who want nothing to do with God, He is going to give them what they want.

Specifically, the Bible says God will accommodate these unbelievers by sending them "strong delusion." In Greek, "strong delusion" is *energeian planes*. The word *energeian* is from the word *energeo*, and it depicts *a force propelling something forward* or *an energy that ignites a process and facilitates it all the way to its conclusion*. The word *plane* pictures *wandering* or *deviant behavior*. It is a form of the Greek word *planao*, which is translated as "deceive" in Matthew 24:4. It means *to leave a solid moral path* and has even been used to depict *an animal that lost its way and could never find its way back home*.

This passage forecasts that at the end of the age many in society at large will embrace lies. They will turn their ears away from the truth and begin listening to philosophies and theories that are not based in Scripture. God will accommodate their desires by allowing them to become *energized by deception.* That is what "strong delusion" means in Greek. It is a picture of society veering so far off track that it will not be able to find its way back home to the truth.

Deception Will Also Run Rampant in the Church

One of the most disturbing aspects about this widespread departure from the truth is that it will also take place in the Church. Returning to Jesus' conversation with His disciples on the Mount of Olives, He said, "For many shall come in my name, saying, I am Christ; and shall deceive many" (Matthew 24:5).

Notice the words "in my name." In Greek, this literally means *on the reputation or strength of my name.* It is a picture of people coming *in the disguise of Jesus' reputation*, and they will be saying, "...I am Christ...." The word "saying" here is a form of the Greek word *legontes*, which means *alleging; claiming*, or *purporting.* And the word "Christ" is *christos* in Greek, which is the word for *the anointing.* Hence, a better translation of this part of the verse would be: "People will come disguised in my reputation claiming to be anointed."

Jesus said these pretenders will "deceive many." The word "deceive" is again the Greek word *planao*, which depicts *delusion* or *a moral wandering.* Specifically, it is *a moral wandering from the foundational doctrines of the Bible, resulting in confusion about what is right or wrong.* This is the delusion that will be at work in society at the end of the age.

The apostle Paul confirms that deception will infiltrate the Church in First Timothy 4:1. Writing under the unction of the Holy Spirit, he said, "Now the Spirit speaketh expressly, that in the latter times some shall depart from the faith, giving heed to seducing spirits, and doctrines of devils."

The word "expressly" in this verse is the Greek word *rhetos*, and it means *explicitly.* It describes something in *undeniable, unmistakable terms.* It is the equivalent of the Holy Spirit raising His voice and speaking emphatically, categorically, and explicitly in the clearest of terms.

What did the Holy Spirit say so strongly through Paul? He declared, "...that in the latter times some shall depart from the faith..." (1 Timothy 4:1). In Greek, the word "latter" is *husteron*, which means *at the very end; at the final conclusion.* And the word "times" is a form of the Greek word *kairos*, which describes *a season of time.* Thus, when we come to the very end of the age, the devil will be at work in the Church causing some to depart from "the faith" — from *the clear, sound teaching of Scripture.*

The phrase "shall depart" is a translation of the Greek word *apistemi*, which means *to change positions*. What is interesting about this word is that it does not mean a rejection or an abandonment of the faith. It is *a slow, methodical departure; a gradual stepping away or withdrawal from the faith to embrace something new and different.* This departure is the result of believers "…giving heed to seducing spirits, and doctrines of devils" (1 Timothy 4:1).

Isn't it amazing that before Jesus ever talked about wars and rumors of wars, kingdoms rising against kingdoms, or earthquakes and famines and pestilence, the first authenticating sign He gave that the end of the age is near is that deception will run rampant — even in the Church. That is why the first thing He said to His disciples — *and us* — is "…Take heed that no man deceive you" (Matthew 24:4). When worldwide deception is taking place, you will know that you've come to the very, very end of the age and Christ is on the verge of coming back.

In our next lesson, we will take a look at the next signs Jesus gave us that mark the end of the age: wars, commotions, and nations and kingdoms against nations and kingdoms.

STUDY QUESTIONS

Study to shew thyself approved unto God, a workman that needeth not to be ashamed, rightly dividing the word of truth.
— 2 Timothy 2:15

1. Jesus said the signs that will precede His coming and the end of the age will be like *birth pains* or *contractions* a woman in labor experiences before having her baby. How does this imagery help you better understand the cataclysmic events we can expect to take place in the last of the last days?

2. The greatest antidote for deception is *feeding your soul and spirit the unchanging truth of God's Word!* According to these passages of Scripture, how will the Word guard you from being deceived?
   - 2 Timothy 3:16,17
   - Psalm 19:7-11

- Psalm 119:9,11
- Proverbs 4:20-22
- John 15:3; 17:17
- Hebrews 4:12
- James 1:21

PRACTICAL APPLICATION

> But be ye doers of the word, and not hearers only, deceiving your own selves.
> —James 1:22

The word "deceive" depicts the behavior of someone who once walked on a solid path but is now drifting and teetering on the edge of a treacherous route. It is going cross grain against all that was once a part of one's core belief system and, sadly, is now deviating from his former solid moral position to a course that is unreliable, unpredictable and even dangerous.

1. In light of this definition, are there any places of your life in which you are deceived? Are there areas in which you've drifted from what was once a solid, biblical belief? If so, where?
2. How have you deviated from the former, time-tested biblical standards and moral positions you once held on to? What were you once doing that you are no longer doing?
3. If God is convicting you, welcome the searchlight of His Holy Spirit in your life. It is because He loves you that He is pointing out the error of your ways and drawing you back to Himself. Repent of any sin and ask Him for the grace to get back on the path of truth.

LESSON 4

TOPIC
Wars, Commotions, Nations and Kingdoms Against Nations and Kingdoms

SCRIPTURES

1. **Matthew 24:3-7** — And as he sat upon the mount of Olives, the disciples came unto him privately, saying, Tell us, when shall these things be? and what shall be the sign of thy coming, and of the end of the world? And Jesus answered and said unto them, Take heed that no man deceive you. For many shall come in my name, saying, I am Christ; and shall deceive many. And ye shall hear of wars and rumours of wars: see that ye be not troubled: for all these things must come to pass, but the end is not yet. For nation shall rise against nation, and kingdom against kingdom…

2. **Luke 21:9** — But when ye shall hear of wars and commotions, be not terrified: for these things must first come to pass; but the end is not by and by.

3. **Philippians 4:7** — And the peace of God, which passeth all understanding, shall keep your hearts and minds through Christ Jesus.

GREEK WORDS

1. "when" — ποτέ (*pote*): specific information; seeking a concrete answer
2. "what" — τι (*ti*): minute, minuscule detail; exactly; explicitly
3. "sign" — σημεῖον (*semeion*): a marker or sign to alert a traveler to where he is on a road; authenticating marks, or specific signs
4. "end" — συντέλειας (*sunteleias*): the closure, summation, or wrap-up of the age
5. "world" — αἰῶνος (*aionos*): not the world itself, but age
6. "hear" — ἀκούω (*akouo*): to hear; acoustics

7. "wars" — πόλεμος (*polemos*): the plural form of a Greek word that describes armed conflicts, which would include battles, fights, skirmishes, and large-scale conflicts
8. "rumors" — ἀκοή (*akoe*): ear; something heard in the ear; hence, rumor
9. "troubled" — θροέω (*throeo*): inward fright that causes one to be filled with worry, anxiety, or fear; worry and inward anxiety resulting from outward events that keep occurring repeatedly
10. "end" — τέλος (*telos*): the ultimate conclusion or climax of a thing
11. "commotions" — ἀκαταστασία (*akatastasia*): instability; out of control; upheaval; anarchy; turbulent upheavals of a societal, political, or militaristic nature
12. "terrified" — πτοέω (*ptoeo*): flutter; inward panic or terror; terrorized; fright that results from something that startles or alarms
13. "nation" — ἔθνος (*ethnos*): nations or ethnic groups; includes various nations, races, colors, or religious groups
14. "against" — ἐπί (*epi*): upon; superiority; pictures a crushing or subjugating force; a force that crushes or smashes; pictures a decimating force
15. "kingdom" — βασιλεία (*basileia*): a kingdom; a sphere of influence; ideology; or even political realm
16. "keep" — φρουρέω (*phroureo*): a military term to express the idea of soldiers who stood faithfully at their post at the city gates to guard and control all who went in and out of the city; the keeping of soldiers who served as gate monitors, whose approval was necessary for anyone to enter the city; used to denote the guarding or keeping of whatever has been entrusted into one's responsibility or care

SYNOPSIS

There is an ancient street that runs alongside the western wall of the temple mount in Jerusalem. It is a road so old that it dates back to the time of Jesus, and it is likely that He and His disciples walked it regularly. In fact, the conversation recorded in Matthew 24 about the end of the age could have begun on this very street.

The Bible says, "Then Jesus went out of the Temple and was walking away when his disciples came up and drew his attention to its buildings. 'You see all these?' replied Jesus. 'I tell you every stone will be thrown down till there is not a single one left standing upon another'" (Matthew 24:1,2 *JB Phillips*). These words shook the disciples to the core and prompted them to begin asking questions.

In the First Century, much like today, people were mesmerized with the subject of prophecy. The disciples' questions back then are quite similar to the questions believers are still asking today. Out of His kindness, compassion, and love, Jesus answered them candidly and clearly. We, who are living in the last of the last days, need to know and understand what Jesus said so we can protect ourselves and our loved ones and sail through these times victoriously.

The emphasis of this lesson:

Wars, rumors of wars, nation rising against nation, and kingdom rising against kingdom are all signs Jesus prophesied would take place before His return and the end of the age. Our last days generation has a nonstop flow of news and information buzzing in our ears, but we are not to be troubled by what we hear. We are to allow the peace of God to guard our hearts and minds in Christ Jesus.

A Review of Our Anchor Verse

Matthew 24:3 records the disciples' response to Jesus' prediction that the temple would be utterly destroyed. It says, "And as he [Jesus] sat upon the mount of Olives, the disciples came unto him privately, saying, Tell us, when shall these things be? and what shall be the sign of thy coming, and of the end of the world?

There are five very important words in this verse: the words when, what, sign, end, and world. In order to really comprehend what the disciples were privately asking Jesus, you have to understand the original Greek meanings of these five words.

The first thing they asked was, "When shall these things be?" In Greek, the word "when" is the word *pote*, and it describes *specific or concrete information*, which means they were not asking for a vague answer. As they were alone with the Lord and no one else was listening, they said, "Lord, while no one else is around, please tell us concretely and specifically when will all these things be?"

Then they said, "What shall be the sign of thy coming?" The word "what" is the little Greek word *ti*, and it describes *the most minute, minuscule detail; something exact or explicit*. Here, the disciples were saying, "Lord, be explicit and exact with us. We want to really comprehend what will be the sign of Your coming — even down to the minute, minuscule details."

The word "sign" in Matthew 24:3 is the Greek word *semeion*, which was the very word used in the First Century to describe *the signs or markers you would see on the road as you were traveling to a new place*. They were intended to tell you where you were on your journey and how much further you had to go to get to your destination. By using the Greek word *semeion* — translated here as "sign" — the disciples were literally saying, "Lord, what will be the authenticating signs we'll see on the prophetic road to the end of the age? What markers should we look for that will tell us where we are on the journey and how much further we have to go before we get to the end of the world?"

This brings us to the word "end," which is the Greek word *sunteleias*. It refers to *the closure, summation*, or *wrap-up of* something. In this case, it is the wrap-up of the world. The word "world" here is the Greek word *aionos*, which is not the world itself but *the current age*. The world will never really end; it will always be here. But eventually this particular age will run its course and be wrapped up, and a new one will begin. The disciples knew this instinctively; it was basic understanding of prophecy.

All that said, the disciples asked Jesus, "Lord, when will we know when this particular age we're living in right now has reached its conclusion? What will be the confirming signs that it is really wrapping up and going to end?"

The First Sign: Worldwide Deception

The first words out of Jesus' mouth after the disciples asked their questions were, "…Take heed that no man deceive you. For many shall come in my name, saying, I am Christ; and shall deceive many" (Matthew 24:4,5). We saw in the last lesson that the first and foremost sign Jesus gave to let us know that we have come to the wrap-up or consummation of the current age is *worldwide deception*. And because people will reject the truth, God will send them a "strong delusion," which in Greek means He will release them to be *energized by deception*.

Not only will the world be deceived, but there will also be deception in the Church. The Bible says some believers will gradually step away from the time-tested truth of Scripture, and it will be the result of them "…giving heed to seducing spirits, and doctrines of devils" (1 Timothy 4:1).

There Will Be 'Wars' and 'Rumors of Wars'

In Matthew 24:6, Jesus went on to say, "And ye shall hear of wars and rumours of wars: see that ye be not troubled: for all these things must come to pass, but the end is not yet." In this verse we are presented with two more specific, concrete signs of the end of the age and Jesus' soon return — *wars* and *rumors of wars*.

When Jesus said, "And ye shall hear," the word "hear" is the Greek word *akouo*, which means *to hear*. It is where we get the word *acoustics*. The word "wars" is the Greek word *polemos*. It is the plural form of a Greek word that describes *armed conflicts*, which would include *battles, fights, skirmishes, and large-scale conflicts*. The fact that this word is plural indicates that there are going to be multiple battles and conflicts occurring simultaneously all across the planet.

Since the turn of the twentieth century, approximately 150 million lives have been lost across the globe as casualties of war. That horrific statistic includes world wars, regional conflicts, and skirmishes in parts of the world renowned for political unrest. We've experienced wars, the threat of wars, and violent disturbances in our cities. Our society has been disrupted by rival governments, fringe militia, factions and groups, and individuals whose hatred drives them to commit unimaginable acts. And these disturbances are no longer lurking in the distance, as they have made their way into our own hometowns and backyards.

Although many wars have been fought throughout human history, Jesus prophesied these events would occur with greater frequency at the very end of the last days. In fact, Jesus gave it as one of the primary signs to let us know when he was about to come again and that the age was concluding.

In addition to wars, Jesus said we would "hear" (*akouo*) of "rumors of wars." The key to understanding this description is in knowing the meaning of the word "rumors." In Greek, it is the word *akoe*, which is the word for *the human ear*. This word is describing *something heard in the ear*; hence, *a rumor*. A last days generation will have an *earful* of news and information about events occurring around the world. That's what this word "rumors" means. It's *an ear buzzing with information.*

Now, Jesus never said we would personally witness all these events. He never said we would personally see the wars or the revolts or the disturbances, but He said we would hear about them. These words of Jesus imply that there will be an excess of information in the last-days generation. The Greek could literally be translated, "You will continually hear and hear and hear and hear," and it presents the idea of *a nonstop flow of information.* And here we see nonstop news being broadcast into our homes and into our ears via television, internet, radio, or other means of communication. Jesus was prophesying that an earful of information will be one of the foremost signs that the finality of the age is approaching.

Don't Be 'Troubled' By What You Hear

Immediately after Jesus alerted us to the occurrence of "wars and rumors of wars," He said, "…See that ye be not troubled: for all these things must come to pass, but the end is not yet" (Matthew 24:6). The word "troubled" in this verse is the Greek word *throeo*, and it describes *an inward fright that causes one to be filled with worry, anxiety, or fear.* It also depicts *worry and inward anxiety resulting from outward events that keep occurring repeatedly.* It could even be translated as *jumpiness* or *nervousness.* Thus, society at the end of the age will be jumpy and nervous because they feel as though they are surrounded on every side by conflicts.

Even with all the wars and rumors of wars, Jesus said, "…The end is not yet" (Matthew 24:6). The word "end" in Greek is the word *telos*, and it describes *the ultimate conclusion or climax of a thing.* This lets us know that even though wars and rumors of wars are major signs that the wrap-up of the age is near, they are not the ultimate sign that we have reached the very, very end of time.

What's interesting is that in Luke's gospel, he reiterates what Jesus said in Matthew 24:6 but adds an additional sign. Luke 21:9 records Jesus as saying, "But when ye shall hear of wars and *commotions*, be not terrified: for these things must first come to pass; but the end is not by and by." The word "commotions" here is the Greek word *akatastasia*, and it describes *instability* or *something that is out of control.* It is the picture of *upheaval, anarchy*, or *turbulent upheavals of a societal, political, or militaristic nature.*

Jesus said that when you hear of instability and societal upheavals of this nature, "...Be not terrified..." (Luke 21:9). In Greek, the word "terrified" is a translation of the word *ptoeo*, which describes an *inward flutter*, an *inward panic*, or *terror*. It means *to be terrorized* and is the very word for *terrorism*. In fact, you could translate this part of the verse, "Be not terrorized."

Here we see Jesus prophesying that as we come to the very end of the age, the unthinkable will begin to take place. Society will be in such an upheaval you will feel as though you're surrounded by anarchy. There will be societal, political, and military upheavals of every kind, and Jesus said these would be another major sign that we're coming to the very end of the age.

Yet, regardless of what is going on, we are not to be filled with inner panic and terror. Jesus said, "...For these things must first come to pass; but the end is not by and by" (Luke 21:9). Again, the word "end" here is the Greek word *telos*, which is the same word used in Matthew 24:6. It describes *the ultimate conclusion or climax of a thing*. Jesus' use of this word lets us know that while "commotions" and "wars" are major signs that the consummation of the age is near, they are not the ultimate sign that we have reached the very, very end of time.

'Nation' Shall Rise Against 'Nation'

When we come to Matthew 24:7, Jesus introduces yet another sign. He said, "For nation shall rise against nation, and kingdom against kingdom...." Notice the word "nation" used twice in this verse. It is the Greek word *ethnos*, which is the word for *nations* or *ethnic groups*. It includes various *nations*, *races*, *colors*, or *religious groups*. Thus, Jesus said that as we near the end of the age, *ethnic groups* will rise up against *ethnic groups* — *races* shall rise up against *races*.

The word "against," which appears twice in Matthew 24:7, is a form of the Greek word *epi*, and it means *upon*. It carries the idea of *superiority* and pictures *a crushing or subjugating force*; *a force that crushes or smashes*; *a decimating force*. The closer we get to the return of Christ and the wrap-up of the age, the more we will see ethnic groups try to crush and decimate other ethnic groups. These types of racial conflicts will escalate and spread across the planet like a disease.

Signs You'll See Just Before Jesus Comes | 35

The reality is, we're seeing this take place all around us. Ethnic tensions have reached an all-time high in our day. Many people have reached an internal boiling point greater than we could have ever imagined. We've also seen a drastic increase in religious groups warring against one another. The Shiite Muslims fighting against the Sunni Muslims is a perfect example. Remember, the word *ethnos* — translated here as "nation" — can also refer to *religious groups*.

'Kingdom' Shall Rise Against 'Kingdom'

But that's not all. Jesus said that "kingdom shall rise against kingdom." The word "kingdom" here is the Greek word *basileia*, and it describes *a kingdom* or *a sphere of influence*. It also denotes *ideology* or *even something in the political realm*.

In this verse, Jesus prophesied that political parties, alliances, and ideological factions will war against each other at the very end of the age, which is exactly what we see happening today. Why is it happening? Because we have an *eyeful* and an *earful of information*. The media itself has been weaponized to perpetuate the assault. Our ears are buzzing with news about all the mudslinging that is happening.

Think about it. Has there ever been a time when people have been more uncivil when it comes to the political realm? We're watching as political parties and affiliations not only try to gain superiority over each other, but also try to decimate and crush each other in the process. There's never been anything like it. It is the clashing of one realm against another realm — one ideology against another ideology. The days of civility are over and will not return because we're in the end of the age.

Everything Jesus said in Matthew 24 is absolutely true. He forecasted that all of these things would take place and continue to increase with greater frequency as we come toward the end of the age.

Through It All, God Will 'Keep' You

The good news is, in spite of all these signs that are happening all around us and will continue to occur to the very end of the age, we do not have to be terrorized by any of it because the peace of God can keep our hearts and minds in Christ Jesus.

Under the inspiration of the Holy Spirit, the apostle Paul wrote, "And the peace of God, which passeth all understanding, shall keep your hearts and minds through Christ Jesus" (Philippians 4:7). The word "keep" in this verse is the Greek word *phroureo*. It is a military term to express the idea of soldiers who stood faithfully at their post at the city gates to guard and control all who went in and out of the city. This word *phroureo* depicts *the keeping of soldiers who served as gate monitors, whose approval was necessary for anyone to enter the city.* It was also used to denote *the guarding or keeping of whatever has been entrusted into one's responsibility or care.*

Paul's use of this word *phroureo* — translated here as "keep" — lets us know that if we will allow the peace of God to do its work in our lives, it will stand guard at the door of our hearts and our minds. And just like those First-Century soldiers stood at the gates of cities and decided who got in and who was denied access, the peace of God will stand at the door of our hearts and minds denying entrance to foul intruders — including all forms of fear, panic, and terror.

At the same time, God's peace will permit access to all that is good, which includes the Word of God, the power of God, the love of God, and the blood of Jesus. God's peace says, "Come on in!" to whatever is honest, whatever is just, whatever is pure, whatever is lovely, whatever is of good report, and whatever is virtuous and worthy of praise (*see* Philippians 4:8). Regardless of what's going on in the world around us, if we have the peace of God operating in our lives, it will keep our hearts and minds in Christ Jesus.

In our next lesson, we will uncover the meaning of several more signs Jesus spoke about, including famine, scarcity, economic woes, pestilence, and diseases.

STUDY QUESTIONS

Study to shew thyself approved unto God, a workman that needeth not to be ashamed, rightly dividing the word of truth.
— 2 Timothy 2:15

If you will let the peace of God do its work in your life, it will stand guard at the door of your heart and mind. Just like those First-Century soldiers, God's peace will determine what is good and godly and allow it to come in, and it will deny access to what is impure and corrupt.

1. Peace is a powerful gift from God and a fruit that His Holy Spirit produces in our lives. Take a moment to reflect on what Jesus said about peace in John 14:27 and 16:33. How do His words encourage you?
2. Many times when God speaks to us, He uses the *presence* or *absence* of peace to direct us. What did the apostle Paul say in Colossians 3:15 about the role of peace in making decisions? If possible, look up this verse in the Amplified Bible and commit it to memory.
3. The key to having and experiencing God's peace that passes all understanding is found in putting into practice Philippians 4:6 and 7. Check out these two verses in a few different Bible versions. Write out the version that leaps off the page and take time to memorize it and make it your own.

PRACTICAL APPLICATION

> But be ye doers of the word, and not hearers only, deceiving your own selves.
> —James 1:22

1. As you listened to and read through the original Greek meaning of what Jesus meant when He said, "And ye shall hear of wars and rumors of wars," what new understanding is the Holy Spirit giving you regarding this passage?
2. In Greek, the word "nation" is *ethnos*, which describes *nations, ethnic groups*, or *religious groups*. Given this original meaning — and that the word "against" describes *a crushing, decimating force* — how has your understanding of "nation rising against nation" been changed by this lesson?
3. Essentially, Jesus said that the last days generation will have *ears buzzing with information* about events occurring all around the world. That's what the word "rumors" means in Matthew 24:6. Knowing that the media itself has been weaponized to perpetuate the assault of rivalry and anarchy in these last days, what practical steps can you take to guard yourself from being swept away by the chaos? (Consider Provers 4:23; Isaiah 26:3,4; Hebrews 12:1-3.)

LESSON 5

TOPIC
Famine, Scarcity, Economic Woes, Pestilence, and Diseases

SCRIPTURES

1. **Matthew 24:3-7** — And as he sat upon the mount of Olives, the disciples came unto him privately, saying, Tell us, when shall these things be? and what shall be the sign of thy coming, and of the end of the world? And Jesus answered and said unto them, Take heed that no man deceive you. For many shall come in my name, saying, I am Christ; and shall deceive many. And ye shall hear of wars and rumours of wars: see that ye be not troubled: for all these things must come to pass, but the end is not yet. For nation shall rise against nation, and kingdom against kingdom: and there shall be famines, and pestilences…

2. **Proverbs 19:17** — He that hath pity upon the poor lendeth unto the Lord; and that which he hath given will he pay him again.

3. **Proverbs 21:13** — Whoso stoppeth his ears at the cry of the poor, he also shall cry himself, but shall not be heard.

4. **Luke 21:11** — And great earthquakes shall be in divers places, and famines, and pestilences….

5. **Psalm 91:1-16** — He that dwelleth in the secret place of the most High shall abide under the shadow of the Almighty. I will say of the Lord, He is my refuge and my fortress: my God; in him will I trust. Surely he shall deliver thee from the snare of the fowler, and from the noisome pestilence. He shall cover thee with his feathers, and under his wings shalt thou trust: his truth shall be thy shield and buckler. Thou shalt not be afraid for the terror by night; nor for the arrow that flieth by day; Nor for the pestilence that walketh in darkness; nor for the destruction that wasteth at noonday. A thousand shall fall at thy side, and ten thousand at thy right hand; but it shall not come nigh thee. Only with thine eyes shalt thou behold and see the reward of the wicked. Because thou hast made the Lord, which is my refuge, even the most High, thy habitation; There shall no evil befall thee, neither

shall any plague come nigh thy dwelling. For he shall give his angels charge over thee, to keep thee in all thy ways. They shall bear thee up in their hands, lest thou dash thy foot against a stone. Thou shalt tread upon the lion and adder: the young lion and the dragon shalt thou trample under feet. Because he hath set his love upon me, therefore will I deliver him: I will set him on high, because he hath known my name. He shall call upon me, and I will answer him: I will be with him in trouble; I will deliver him, and honour him. With long life will I satisfy him, and shew him my salvation.

GREEK WORDS

1. "when" — ποτέ (*pote*): specific information; seeking a concrete answer
2. "what" — τι (*ti*): minute, minuscule detail; exactly; explicitly
3. "sign" — σημεῖον (*semeion*): a marker or sign to alert a traveler to where he is on a road; authenticating marks, or specific signs
4. "end" — συντέλειας (*sunteleias*): the closure, summation, or wrap-up of the age
5. "world" — αἰῶνος (*aionos*): not the world itself, but age
6. "famines" — λιμός (*limos*): plural, multiple famines; a scarcity of grain; deficits of all types, including financial deficits and shortages
7. "pestilence" — λοιμός (*loimos*): plural, pestilences; old diseases being reactivated or newly emerging diseases never seen before

SYNOPSIS

As we noted in our previous lesson, there is an ancient road that runs parallel to the western wall of the temple mount in the city of Jerusalem, and it is so old it dates back to the time of Christ. Everyone in the First Century used this road to go into and out of the temple — including Jesus and His disciples.

One of the most intriguing things about this road today is that there is a huge hole right in the middle of it, and it has been there for nearly 2,000 years. In 70 AD, when Emperor Titus and the Roman army attacked the city of Jerusalem, they destroyed the temple, pulling down all of its stones, many of which toppled down onto this ancient road, breaking the pavement.

Who would have ever imagined that the massive stones that once made up the colossal temple built by King Herod the Great would ever be pried loose and thrown down? But that is exactly what happened, and it is exactly what Jesus prophesied in Matthew 24:2. This enormous pile of stones that is still visible today is proof that everything Jesus said in Matthew 24 will take place.

Before we examine four additional signs Jesus told us we would see as we approach the end of the age, let's briefly review our anchor verse and what we've learned in the first four lessons.

The emphasis of this lesson:

Famines and pestilences are also authenticating signs that Jesus said we will see before His return and the end of the age. Specifically, these words depict worldwide hunger and financial instability along with widespread breakouts of old and new diseases.

A Summary of Our Anchor Verse

In Matthew 24, Jesus is talking with His disciples, and in verse 3 the Bible says, "And as he sat upon the mount of Olives, the disciples came unto him privately, saying, Tell us, when shall these things be? and what shall be the sign of thy coming, and of the end of the world?" Here is a quick overview of five important words in this verse that you need to understand:

WHEN: The disciples asked Jesus, "When shall these things be?"

The word "when" here is the Greek word *pote*, and it describes *specific information* or *a concrete answer*. The disciples were asking Jesus for *specific, concrete information* regarding "when" the temple would be destroyed, "when" He was coming back, and "when" the end of the world would be.

WHAT: The disciples asked Jesus, "What shall be the sign of thy coming?"

The word "what" here is a translation of the little Greek word *ti*, which describes *the most minute, minuscule detail*. The use of this word is the equivalent of the disciples saying, "Lord, tell us *exactly* and *explicitly*, down to the smallest detail, what the sign of Your coming will be."

SIGN: The disciples asked Jesus for a "sign."

The Greek word for "sign" in Matthew 24:3 is the word *semeion*, and it describes *a marker or sign to alert a traveler to where he is on a road*. It is an *authenticating mark*, or *specific sign* that tells a person where he is. These signs change the closer and closer one gets to his destination. The use of this word is the equivalent of the disciples saying, "Lord, what will be the authenticating markers that we'll see on the prophetic road to the end of the world? Tell us what we should look for so we're able to know where we are prophetically in time."

END: The disciples wanted to know when the "end" would be.

The word "end" here is the Greek word *sunteleias*, which describes *the closure, summation, or wrap-up of something*. The insertion of this word tells us that the disciples had a basic prophetic understanding that everything would eventually run its course and come to an end.

WORLD: The disciples asked Jesus, "When is the end of the world?"

The word "world" is the Greek word *aionos*, which does not describe the world, the earth, or the universe. The word *aionos* describes *an age*. Basically, the disciples were asking Jesus, "Lord, how will we know when everything in this age is about to wrap up and You are about to come back? Tell us explicitly and exactly what the authenticating signs will be."

How Did Jesus Respond to the Disciples' Questions?

In Matthew 24:4-7, the Bible says, "And Jesus answered and said unto them, Take heed that no man deceive you. For many shall come in my name, saying, I am Christ; and shall deceive many. And ye shall hear of wars and rumours of wars: see that ye be not troubled: for all these things must come to pass, but the end is not yet. For nation shall rise against nation, and kingdom against kingdom…"

In these four verses, there are nine specific signs Jesus declared we will see prior to His return and before this age comes to an end. These signs are:

1. Worldwide deception (Matthew 24:4)
2. Deception in the Church (Matthew 24:5)
3. Wars (Matthew 24:6)
4. Rumors of wars (Matthew 24:6)
5. Commotions (Luke 21:9)
6. Widespread terrorism (Luke 21:9)

7. Warring political systems (Matthew 24:7)
8. Clash of culture (Matthew 24:7)
9. Ethnic conflicts (Matthew 24:7)

For a detailed review of these authenticating markers, please refer back to Lessons 3 and 4.

Jesus Said There Will Be 'Famines'

Speaking prophetically, Jesus went on to say, "…And there shall be famines, and pestilences…" (Matthew 24:7). Notice He said "shall be." He was pointing into the future, to the very end of the age, and forecasting that there will be "famines." In Greek, the word "famines" is the word *limos*, and it is plural, indicating *multiple famines*. It specifically describes *a scarcity of grain* as well as *deficits of all types*, including *financial deficits and shortages*.

Thus, one of the authenticating signs that the age is wrapping up and Christ is about to return is that there will be multiple "famines" and food scarcities in various parts of the world. Hence, there will be massive hunger across the globe. Currently, there are nearly eight billion people living on the planet, and statistically speaking, one out of nine individuals are suffering from chronic undernourishment.

What makes matters worse is that this condition of malnutrition produces poor health, and when a person has poor health, they can't work. The inability to work leads to poverty, and poverty leads to hunger. Hunger then leads to more poverty, and the vicious cycle continues. This debilitating dilemma is designed by the devil to steal, to kill, and to destroy people's lives. Indeed, poverty and hunger are a horrible combination, and it is clear why God hates it and why Jesus came to break the spirit of poverty in people's lives.

Added to this issue are the growing number of displaced people who have been ousted from their land because of wars and rumors of wars and kingdom rising against kingdom. Of course this only perpetuates the problem of people being out of work and having no money to buy food.

What is interesting about this Greek word *limos* — translated here as "famines" — is that it can also describe an *economic shaking*. Remember, the word *limos* actually describes *a scarcity of grain*. In the First Century, when Jesus was speaking and alerting us to the signs of the end of the age, economies were largely based on grain. If there was a famine of grain, it would often lead to nationwide financial instability and chaos.

Egypt, for example, was rich because it had an abundance of grain. However, if Egypt experienced a famine of grain, it would literally shake the economic world of the First Century. Keep in mind, when you look at this word "famines" in Matthew 24:7, it is really describing an end-time economic shaking. Jesus was forecasting monetary shortfalls and deficits that would affect the global economy at the very end of the age. He was predicting financial instability, economic shortages, and financial hardships that will affect various parts of the Earth before He returns and this present age wraps up.

How Can You Help?

Now you're probably thinking, *How am I to respond to this dilemma? What can I do to help ease the pain of hurting, hungry people across the globe?* As believers, God gives us some very specific direction in this area. For instance, the Bible says, "He that hath pity upon the poor lendeth unto the Lord; and that which he hath given will he pay him again" (Proverbs 19:17). And Second Corinthians 9:9 says, "…The godly man gives generously to the poor. His good deeds will be an honor to him forever."

As Christians, we have a responsibility to hear the cry of the poor and answer. Proverbs 21:13 says, "Whoso stoppeth his ears at the cry of the poor, he also shall cry himself, but shall not be heard." Although we cannot help everyone who is poor, we can each help someone. Think about it: the cost of a hamburger, a side of fries, and a soft drink is the equivalent of what it would take to feed a few people for an entire week in other parts of the world.

Do you really want to touch the heart of God? Would you really like to make a difference in the lives of others now and for eternity? Consider denying yourself eating out one meal a week and investing that money into a ministry that has a proven track record of feeding the hungry and ministering to the needs of those who are in jeopardy because of malnourishment and poverty. When you give to the poor, you are literally giving to the Lord!

Worldwide 'Pestilences' Will Also Be a Sign

As we have noted, three of the four gospels include the conversation Jesus had with His disciples regarding the signs we would see at the end of the age. For instance, what Jesus said in Matthew 24:7 is also found in Luke 21:11. It says, "And great earthquakes shall be in divers places, and famines, and pestilences…."

In this verse, we see the addition of the word "pestilences," which in Greek is the word *loimos*. It is plural in form, indicating *multiple pestilences*. This is a medical term that describes *disease*. Specifically, this word denotes *old diseases being reactivated* or *newly emerging diseases never seen before*. Essentially, Jesus was prophesying that at the end of the age when everything is being wrapped up, numerous diseases — both old and new — will begin to emerge all across the planet.

Today, there are normal strains of infectious diseases raging everywhere. Here are some recent findings from the World Health Organization's website:

> "In this stage of history, professionals predict that directly before us will be the emergence of new infectious diseases and that the reemergence of 'old' diseases will have a significant impact on health. A number of factors will influence this development: travel and trade, microbiological resistance, human behavior, breakdowns in health systems, and increased pressure on the environment. Social, political, and economic factors that cause the movement of people will increase contact between people and microbes, and environmental changes caused by human activity all will contribute to the spread of disease. The overuse of antibiotics and insecticides, combined with inadequate or deteriorating public health infrastructures, will hamper or delay responses to increasing disease threats."

The fact is, this word "pestilences," which refers to *outbreaks of old and new diseases*, could also be classified as *pandemics*. As we have recently witnessed firsthand, pandemics have the potential of affecting the population of whole countries and the world itself.

As believers, how are we to respond to such an overwhelming prediction? The answer is to know what the Bible has to say about healing and walking in divine health. When the enemy tries to instill fear and panic in your heart, run to the Lord! Proverbs 18:10 (*NKJV*) declares, "The name of the Lord is a strong tower; the righteous run to it and are safe."

Friend, our finest hour to shine for Jesus is when the darkness of disease is attempting to destroy lives. In those moments, we are to move in God's wisdom and stay filled with the empowerment of His Holy Spirit (*see* Ephesians 5:18). He will lead us and show us what to do. Our job is to know His Word and take authority over sickness and disease in the mighty name of Jesus!

Get Well-Acquainted With the Promises of Psalm 91

One of the most powerful passages in Scripture that declares the supernatural protection of God is **Psalm 91**. It has been a lifeline for countless individuals from all walks of life for thousands of years. Take a few moments to slowly read through and meditate on this encouraging chapter:

1. He that dwelleth in the secret place of the most High shall abide under the shadow of the Almighty.
2. I will say of the Lord, He is my refuge and my fortress: my God; in him will I trust.
3. Surely he shall deliver thee from the snare of the fowler, and from the noisome pestilence.
4. He shall cover thee with his feathers, and under his wings shalt thou trust: his truth shall be thy shield and buckler.
5. Thou shalt not be afraid for the terror by night; nor for the arrow that flieth by day;
6. Nor for the pestilence that walketh in darkness; nor for the destruction that wasteth at noonday.
7. A thousand shall fall at thy side, and ten thousand at thy right hand; but it shall not come nigh thee.
8. Only with thine eyes shalt thou behold and see the reward of the wicked.
9. Because thou hast made the Lord, which is my refuge, even the most High, thy habitation;
10. There shall no evil befall thee, neither shall any plague come nigh thy dwelling.

11. For he shall give his angels charge over thee, to keep thee in all thy ways.
12. They shall bear thee up in their hands, lest thou dash thy foot against a stone.
13. Thou shalt tread upon the lion and adder: the young lion and the dragon shalt thou trample under feet.
14. Because he hath set his love upon me, therefore will I deliver him: I will set him on high, because he hath known my name.
15. He shall call upon me, and I will answer him: I will be with him in trouble; I will deliver him, and honour him.
16. With long life will I satisfy him, and shew him my salvation.

Part of God's "salvation" mentioned in verse 16 is the provision of His health and healing. In Exodus 15:26, God said, "…I am the Lord that healeth thee," and in First Peter 2:24 we see that by the broken body of Jesus Christ — His "stripes" — we are healed. As a child of God, healing and wholeness are yours. No, you don't deserve it and you cannot earn it. It is God's gift to you through Jesus, and it is received by faith.

In our next lesson, we will examine more signs Jesus predicted we would see as we approach the end of the age, including catastrophic events, monstrous developments, and signs from the heavens.

STUDY QUESTIONS

Study to shew thyself approved unto God, a workman that needeth not to be ashamed, rightly dividing the word of truth.
— 2 Timothy 2:15

1. God is mindful of the poor, and He wants us to be mindful of them as well. Look at how He promises to bless you as you are faithful to remember and give to those in need:

   - Psalm 41:1
   - Proverbs 14:21; 19:17
   - Proverbs 22:9; 28:27
   - Matthew 19:21; Luke 12:33
   - Luke 6:38; Proverbs 11:25; Galatians 6:8-10

2. The Bible says, "...Faith and works, works and faith, fit together hand in glove" (James 2:18 *MSG*). Take a few moments to read these sobering words from James, John and Jesus regarding helping those in need:
   - James 2:15-18
   - 1 John 3:17,18
   - Matthew 25:34-40

   What is God speaking to you through these passages?

PRACTICAL APPLICATION

> **But be ye doers of the word, and not hearers only, deceiving your own selves.**
> **—James 1:22**

1. To combat the outbreak of pestilences in these last days, you need to know what the Bible says about healing and walking in divine health. What scriptures do you know, and possibly can even quote by heart, that declare the power of God's healing for you and your family?

2. God Himself has said, "...He that hath my word, let him speak my word faithfully..." (Jeremiah 23:28). To help build your faith and arm yourself with ammunition from God's Word, check out these promises on healing and divine health from Scripture and begin making them a part of your prayers for yourself, for your family, and for others.
   - 3 John 2
   - Proverbs 4:20-22
   - Psalm 91:1-7
   - Isaiah 53:4,5; 1 Peter 2:24
   - Exodus 15:26; 23:25,26
   - James 5:14,15

3. Do you really want to touch the heart of God and make a difference in the lives of others, now and for eternity? Take a little time to do some research and find out what reputable ministries and organizations are providing food for the poor locally and around the world. Then pray: *"Lord, what would You like me and my family to do? Who*

would You like me to support, and how much would You like us to give?" Listen carefully to what He says and begin to do it by faith.

LESSON 6

TOPIC

Catastrophic Events, Monstrous Developments, Signs From the Heavens

SCRIPTURES

1. **Matthew 24:3-7** — And as he sat upon the mount of Olives, the disciples came unto him privately, saying, Tell us, when shall these things be? and what shall be the sign of thy coming, and of the end of the world? And Jesus answered and said unto them, Take heed that no man deceive you. For many shall come in my name, saying, I am Christ; and shall deceive many. And ye shall hear of wars and rumours of wars: see that ye be not troubled: for all these things must come to pass, but the end is not yet. For nation shall rise against nation, and kingdom against kingdom: and there shall be famines, and pestilences, and earthquakes, in divers places.

2. **Luke 21:11** — And great earthquakes shall be in divers places, and famines, and pestilences; and fearful sights and great signs shall there be from heaven.

3. **Romans 8:22** — For we know that the whole creation groaneth and travaileth in pain together until now.

GREEK WORDS

1. "when" — ποτέ (*pote*): specific information; seeking a concrete answer
2. "what" — τι (*ti*): minute, minuscule detail; exactly; explicitly
3. "sign" — σημεῖον (*semeion*): a marker or sign to alert a traveler to where he is on a road; authenticating marks, or specific signs
4. "end" — συντέλειας (*sunteleias*): the closure, summation, or wrap-up of the age

5. "world" — αἰῶνος (*aionos*): not the world itself, but age
6. "earthquakes" — σεισμός (*seismos*): plural, multiple earthquakes; a lot of seismic activity
7. "great earthquakes" — σεισμοί τε μεγάλοι (*seismoi te megaloi*): great earthquakes; great seismic activity
8. "fearful sights" — φόβητρον (*phobetron*): monstrous events; scary events; used by ancient Greeks to describe monsters
9. "great signs shall there be from heaven" — ἀπ' οὐρανοῦ σημεῖα μεγάλα ἔσται (*ap' ouranou semeia mgala estai*): there will be great signs directly from heaven

SYNOPSIS

The Old Testament and the New Testament are filled with Bible prophecy, and a great deal of this prophecy is connected with the nation of Israel and the city of Jerusalem. However, there are also prophecies that deal explicitly with society and the world as a whole.

The apostle Paul gives one such prophecy in Second Timothy 3 as he vividly describes the bizarre mindsets that are going to develop in the thinking of society as we come closer to the very end of the age. When we look at what Paul says in this chapter along with the specific signs Jesus tells us we're going to see as we draw closer to His return, it's plain to see that God has chosen us to live in the very end of the age.

So how are we supposed to respond to all these strange developments that are happening all around us? How are we to live in a world that's spinning out of control — a world that is failing morally and headed toward catastrophic events? God has not called us to be filled with fear and take on the depressed, defeated attitude of the rest of the world. Instead, He wants us to get into His Word and know — *really know* — how to thrive in any situation in which we find ourselves. Remember, through Christ He has made us more than conquerors! (*See* Romans 8:37.)

The emphasis of this lesson:

Jesus prophesied in Matthew 24:7 and Luke 21:11 that in the last of the last days, increased seismic activity will take place globally and a vast number of earthquakes will be felt in various places all across the earth. This is a major sign that Christ's return is near.

A Review of Our Anchor Verse

As we have seen in each of the previous lessons, Matthew 24 captures a candid conversation between Jesus and His disciples regarding the last days. When we come to verse 3, the Bible says, "And as he [Jesus] sat upon the mount of Olives, the disciples came unto him privately, saying, Tell us, when shall these things be? and what shall be the sign of thy coming, and of the end of the world?" There are five very important words in this verse, and they are the words *when, what, sign, end,* and *world*.

The first thing the disciples asked was, "When shall these things be?" In Greek, the word **"when"** is the word *pote*, and it describes *specific or concrete information*, which means the disciples were not asking for a vague answer. Rather, they were saying, "Lord tell us *concretely* and *exactly* when shall these things be?"

Then they said, "What shall be the sign of thy coming?" The word **"what"** is the Greek word *ti*, and it describes *the most minute, minuscule detail; something exact or explicit*. Here, the disciples were saying, "Lord, speak *plainly* and *explicitly* to us. We really want to understand what will be the sign of Your coming — even down to the *minute, minuscule details*."

The word **"sign"** in Matthew 24:3 is the Greek word *semeion*, which was the very word used in the First Century to describe *the signs or markers you would see on the road as you were traveling to a new place*. Those signs were there to tell you where you were on your journey and how much further you had to go before you reached your destination. In this case, the disciples were asking, "Lord, where are we on God's prophetic timeclock? How much further do we have to go? If we're actually on the road to the end of the world, what are the authenticating markers that will confirm it?"

This brings us to the word **"end,"** which is the Greek word *sunteleias*. It refers to *the closure, summation*, or *wrap-up of something*. In this case, it is the wrap-up of the world.

Unfortunately, the word **"world"** here is a poor translation, because it does not describe the earth or the universe. Here, the word "world" is the Greek word *aionos*, which describes *the current age*. The fact is, the world will never end; it will always be here. But eventually the current age we're in will run its course and be wrapped up, and a new age will begin. The disciples knew this instinctively; it was a basic understanding of prophecy.

Hence, the disciples basically asked Jesus, "Lord, what are the signs we're going to see as we journey down this prophetic road that explicitly tells us we have come to the wrap-up of this age?"

Jesus Pointed to Multiple Signs We'd See Before His Return and the End of the Age

It is interesting to note that in Matthew 24:3, the disciples asked Jesus for *one* sign — or *the* sign — that would emphatically mark His return and the end of the age. Rather than just giving them one, Jesus gave His disciples — *and us* — numerous authenticating markers that would confirm His coming and the wrap-up of the age was near. The Bible says:

> **And Jesus answered and said unto them, Take heed that no man deceive you.**
>
> **Matthew 24:4**

When most people read Matthew 24, they read right over this verse, but it is one of the most important verses of all. In it, Jesus gives the first and foremost sign that we've come to the very end of the age. By warning us to guard against being deceived, He is telling us that deception will be widespread across the globe at the end of the age. The apostle Paul called this "strong delusion" (*see* 2 Thessalonians 2:11).

Jesus continued in the next verse saying that this "strong delusion" will even try to find its way into the Church.

> **For many shall come in my name, saying, I am Christ; and shall deceive many.**
>
> **Matthew 24:5**

For a detailed review of worldwide deception and deception in the Church, refer back to Lesson 3.

Jesus went on to describe two more major signs before the end of the age in verse 6:

> **And ye shall hear of wars and rumours of wars: see that ye be not troubled: for all these things must come to pass, but the end is not yet.**
>
> **Matthew 24:6**

Then immediately after notifying us that there would be wars and rumors of wars, Jesus said,

> **For nation shall rise against nation, and kingdom against kingdom...**
> — Matthew 24:7

We saw that in the Greek, the word "nation" is the word *ethnos*, which describes *ethnic groups* or *religious groups*. And the word "kingdom" is the Greek word *basileia*, which describes *ideology* or even a *political realm*. Thus, as we continue to move toward to the end of the age, *ethnic groups* will rise up against *ethnic groups*, *religious groups* will rise up against *religious groups*, and one *political ideology* will rise up against another *political ideology*.

The word "against," which appears twice in this verse, is the Greek word *epi*, and it carries the idea of *superiority* or *mastery over another*. It pictures *a crushing or subjugating force*; *a force that crushes or smashes*; *a decimating force*. Thus, the closer we get to the return of Christ and the wrap-up of the age, the more we will see ethnic groups trying to crush and decimate other ethnic groups. These types of racial conflicts will escalate and spread across the planet like a disease. For a detailed review of these signs found in Matthew 24:6 and 7, refer back to Lesson 4.

Then in our last lesson, we learned about two more last-days signs that Jesus predicted. He said,

> **...And there shall be famines, and pestilences....**
> — Matthew 24:7

In Greek, the word "famines" depicts *worldwide hunger* and *financial instability*, and the word "pestilences" in Greek is a medical term that refers to *widespread breakouts of old and new diseases*. Jesus prophesied that famines and pestilences will be two authenticating signs that we will see before His return and before the end of the age.

'Earthquakes in Divers Places' Is Another Major End-Times Sign

The next sign Christ said we would see at the end of the age is "...earthquakes, in divers places" (Matthew 24:7). In Greek, the word "earthquakes" is the word *seismos*, which is where we get the words *seismic activity* and *seismograph*. Here the word *seismos* is plural, indication *multiple earthquakes; a lot of seismic activity*.

Because the word "earthquakes" — the Greek word *seismos* — is used in the plural form here, it emphatically tells us Jesus was predicting a time of prolific, seismic activity that will occur at the end of the age. Luke also wrote about this in Luke 21:11, saying, "And great earthquakes shall be in divers places...." The words "great earthquakes" in Greek literally means *great seismic activity*. The word "great" in the original language can depict *something large in size* or it can mean *numerous in quantity*. Furthermore, Jesus stated that these "earthquakes" will occur in "divers places," which means the earth will be touched globally by increased seismic activity towards the end of the age.

The scientific record today demonstrates that earthquakes are part of the earth's geological history. But Jesus was not giving a geological history of the earth when He spoke these words. He was prophesying about the future in Matthew 24:7 and Luke 21:11. In both places, Jesus said there "*shall be*" earthquakes. He was pointing to the very end of the age and forecasting what will happen in a condensed period of time at the very end of the last days.

Therefore, according to Jesus, increased seismic activity will take place globally, and a vast number of earthquakes will be felt in various places across the earth. That is exactly what we are experiencing in the world today. Our Earth is trembling. The U.S. Geological Survey currently estimates *several million* earthquakes occur every year. Although many of them are undetected because they occur in remote locations, millions of earthquakes are occurring annually nonetheless just like Jesus said.

And today, because of advanced scientific equipment, we're able to measure the intensity of many earthquakes and determine that the number of earthquakes has steadily increased since scientists began recording and analyzing seismic activity.

In Luke's gospel Jesus clearly stated there would be "great earthquakes" as the time of His return approaches, and that's what we're seeing. Hence, we can infer from this verse of scripture that the word "great" may mean *great quantities* of earthquakes and seismic activity.

This prophecy ties into what the apostle Paul said in Romans 8:22: "For we know that the whole creation groaneth and travaileth in pain together until now." Amazingly, even the planet knows that this present age is ending and another one is about to be birthed. Each earthquake is like another contraction. And like a pregnant woman who is in labor and about to deliver her child, the earth is groaning and travailing (laboring), waiting for the manifestation — or the birthing — of the sons and daughters of God.

The Last Days Generation Will See 'Fearful Sights'

Looking once more at Luke 21:11, Jesus said, "And great earthquakes shall be in divers places, and famines, and pestilences; and fearful sights and great signs shall there be from heaven." Notice the words "fearful sights." This is a translation of the unusual Greek word *phobetron*, and it describes *monstrous events* or *scary events*.

In all honesty, the words "fearful sights" are a mystery. This phrase comes from a Greek word that depicts *fright, horror or something that is scary*. Greek writers usually used this word to describe *monsters*. So these words conjure up horrific images and feelings of dread and horror. What Jesus was referring to in Luke 21:11 is not exactly clear, but whatever these words mean to a last-days society, Jesus said they would be *monstrous* in the eyes of God and to the minds of men.

One possibility is that this phrase refers to some form of cataclysmic, natural disaster. It's interesting to note that when Jesus prophesied about the very end of the last days, He specifically listed several types of natural disasters by name, which might indicate that this additional warning of "fearful sights" refers to something else entirely because it's not specific.

One previously unimaginable possibility has arisen. Because of scientific and technological advancements, there are so many new developments that something horrific could be unleashed in our times. Possibly Jesus was referring to something of a scientific nature. It is sufficient to say that there are many different scenarios one could imagine that would fall under the umbrella of Jesus' warning about "fearful sights." Any ideas will remain firmly in the realm of conjecture because Jesus purposefully kept this warning vague. Nevertheless, one thing is clear — as a child of God, we do not need to be afraid of anything that is coming in the future. We have the Word of God, the power of God, and the blood of Jesus. And we're going to be alright.

There Will Also Be 'Great Signs From Heaven'

There was one other thing Jesus said we would see in Luke 21:11 and it was "…great signs shall there be from heaven." The word "great" here is a form of the Greek word *mega*, and it describes *something that will have a mega impact on the population of the earth*. It is *something that is monumental, far-reaching, and deeply impacting on the earth and its population.*

And whatever these "great signs" are, Jesus said they will come *directly from Heaven*. That is what this phrase literally says in the Greek — *from the heavens* or *something descending directly from the sky*. Therefore, the majority of the human race will be aware of it when it takes place, and when these great signs come from the heavens, they will tell us we are on the precipice of the very, very end of this age and the beginning of the next age.

Now you may ask, "What exactly are these great signs we're going to see from the heavens?" Again, Jesus was not clear on what it is. It may be a mammoth meteor or an asteroid. It also might be a solar flare. And there is always the possibility that it is something we've never really considered before. Whatever it is, Jesus emphatically said it will be "great" — from the Greek word *mega* — and it will have a *mega impact* on the population of the world. It will come directly from the heavens and will be a *monstrous, horrific* experience to those who witness it.

Thus, at the very wrap-up of the age just before Jesus returns to rapture the Church, He said there will be great earthquakes all over the earth. They will be like the contractions of a woman in labor ready to give birth to her child. Jesus said there will also be monstrous events or signs taking place in the sky and descending to the earth. Our generation is going to see things in the heavens on a global scale that no other generation has ever seen before. When you see all of these things happening, wake up, hold your head high, and look up to the sky because your redemption is drawing near. Jesus is about to come again!

In our next lesson, we will see how widespread persecution that will come to the Church is another major sign that the end of the age is drawing near.

STUDY QUESTIONS

> Study to shew thyself approved unto God, a workman that needeth not to be ashamed, rightly dividing the word of truth.
> — 2 Timothy 2:15

The apostle Paul said, "It is plain to anyone with eyes to see that at the present time all created life groans in a sort of universal travail" (Romans 8:22 *JB Phillips*). We know from our study that the earth's travail is like the contractions of an expectant mother in labor.

1. According to Romans 8:20, why has creation been subjected to death and decay?

   (Also *consider* Genesis 3:17,18 and Romans 5:12.)

2. What does Romans 8:19 say that all of creation is waiting to see?

3. What miracle did Paul prophesy is going to occur in nature in Romans 8:21?

   (Also *see* Second Peter 3:13 and Revelation 21:1,5.)

PRACTICAL APPLICATION

> But be ye doers of the word, and not hearers only, deceiving your own selves.
> — James 1:22

1. Jesus predicted a time of prolific, seismic activity will occur at the end of the age. For an eye-opening look at just how many earthquakes have occurred over the past few decades — and in the recent year — check out earthquake.usgs.gov and the interactive earthquake map at seismo.berkeley.edu. How does seeing this scientific data confirm Jesus' prophetic words and excite you about His soon appearance?

2. According to Jesus, the last days generation is going to see "fearful sights and great signs" from heaven (*see* Luke 21:11). Prior to this teaching, had you ever heard that such events were coming? Why do you think Jesus left this particular sign as a mystery?

LESSON 7

TOPIC
Worldwide Persecution

SCRIPTURES

1. **Matthew 24:3-10** — And as he sat upon the mount of Olives, the disciples came unto him privately, saying, Tell us, when shall these things be? and what shall be the sign of thy coming, and of the end of the world? And Jesus answered and said unto them, Take heed that no man deceive you. For many shall come in my name, saying, I am Christ; and shall deceive many. And ye shall hear of wars and rumours of wars: see that ye be not troubled: for all these things must come to pass, but the end is not yet. For nation shall rise against nation, and kingdom against kingdom: and there shall be famines, and pestilences, and earthquakes, in divers places. All these are the beginning of sorrows. Then shall they deliver you up to be afflicted, and shall kill you: and ye shall be hated of all nations for my name's sake. And then shall many be offended, and shall betray one another, and shall hate one another.

2. **Luke 21:16,17** — And ye shall be betrayed both by parents, and brethren, and kinsfolks, and friends; and some of you shall they cause to be put to death. And ye shall be hated of all men for my name's sake.

3. **Luke 21:12-15** — ...They shall lay their hands on you, and persecute you, delivering you up to the synagogues, and into prisons, being brought before kings and rulers for my name's sake. And it [this situation of persecutions] shall turn to you for a testimony. Settle it therefore in your hearts, not to meditate before what ye shall answer: For I will give you a mouth and wisdom, which all your adversaries shall not be able to gainsay nor resist.

GREEK WORDS

1. "when" — **ποτέ** (*pote*): specific information; seeking a concrete answer
2. "what" — **τι** (*ti*): minute, minuscule detail; exactly; explicitly

3. "sign" — σημεῖον (*semeion*): a marker or sign to alert a traveler to where he is on a road; authenticating marks, or specific signs
4. "end" — συντέλειας (*sunteleias*): the closure, summation, or wrap-up of the age
5. "world" — αἰῶνος (*aionos*): not the world itself, but age
6. "afflicted" — θλῖψις (*thlipsis*): affliction; tribulation; trouble; great pressure; crushing pressure; suffocating pressure; a horribly tight, life-threatening squeeze
7. "kill" — ἀποκτείνω (*apokteino*): slaughter; massacre; butcher; ruthlessly kill; torture; outright slaughter; can denote the giving of a death sentence
8. "hated" — μισέω (*miseo*): hate; abhor; utterly repulsive; a deep-seated animosity; intense hatred; repugnance; objectionable; something that causes one to feel disgust, repulsion; a deep-seated aversion; not just a case of dislike; it is a case of actual hatred
9. "offended" — σκανδαλίζω (*skandalidzo*): scandal; scandalous; offend
10. "betray" — παραδίδωμι (*paradidomi*): to deliver or to hand something over to someone else; to betray by delivering
11. "persecute" — διώκω (*dioko*): to hunt, to chase, or to pursue; to persecute; denotes the actions of a hunter who followed after an animal in order to apprehend, to capture to kill it; to strategically follow after an object, principle, or person until it is captured and caught; entrapment
12. "synagogue" — συναγωγή (*sunagoge*): synagogue; synagogues were also places where court judgments were issued by Jewish officials to those found guilty of a crime; the word "synagogue" here corresponds with the idea of a court system
13. "prisons" — φυλακή (*phulake*): a place of custody, a jail where one serves a sentence that has been rendered for his or her alleged offense

SYNOPSIS

The city of Jerusalem is a beautiful historic location where many of the events of the Bible took place and where many more future events are going to occur according to Bible prophecy. Actually, if we carefully examine all the Scriptures, we would find that nearly one-third of them fall into the category of prophecy.

The word "prophecy" basically means *something spoken in advance* or *foretold*. Clearly, the Bible foretells many things that are coming in the future, including the condition of the world in the last days and the signs we can expect to see before Jesus returns and this present age wraps up. In view of the current state of society and the Church, it seems certain that we are in fact living in the last of the last days.

It's no accident that you're alive during this incredible period of history. According to Acts 17:26, God purposely chose you to live on earth right now, at the very end of this age. That being the case, you need to know what the Bible says about this era so that you can navigate the times and keep your family and yourself protected.

The emphasis of this lesson:

Before Christ's return, the Church will experience persecution in various forms and in various places around the world, including the overwhelming pressure of affliction, deep-seated hatred, betrayal, imprisonment, and in some cases death.

A Review of Our Anchor Verse

In Matthew 24:2, Jesus prophesied to His disciples that the magnificent temple in Jerusalem would one day be pulled apart and not one stone would be left in its place. Alarmed by Jesus' words, the disciples looked for an opportunity to speak with Him alone to find out what He meant. The Bible says, "And as he [Jesus] sat upon the mount of Olives, the disciples came unto him privately, saying, Tell us, when shall these things be? and what shall be the sign of thy coming, and of the end of the world?" (Matthew 24:3)

We've seen that the word "when" is the Greek word *pote*, and it describes *very specific information*. It lets us know the disciples were saying, "Lord, don't be vague with us — give us *a concrete answer*. We want to know exactly when all these things are going to take place and what shall be the sign of thy coming?"

The word "what" in Greek is the little word *ti*, and it describes *the most minute, minuscule detail*. This word tells us that the disciples got very specific and said, "Lord tell us *exactly* and *explicitly* — down to the very smallest detail — what shall be the sign of thy coming?"

We have noted that the word "sign" is the Greek word *semeion*, which is the very word that was used to describe *the markers or signs a traveler saw as he was traveling on a road to a new destination*. Those signs were designed to tell travelers exactly where they were in their journey and how much further they had to go before reaching their destination.

By using this word *semeion* (sign), the disciples were saying, "Lord, what are the *authenticating signs* we're going to see on this prophetic road to tell us exactly where we are on God's prophetic calendar and how close we are to the end of the world?"

In this verse, the word "world" is a poor translation. It is the Greek word *aionos*, and it would better be translated *age*. Hence, it is *the end of the age*. The fact is, the world is never going to end, but it will transition into a new age and be changed. The disciples understood prophetically that this current age would eventually run its course and come to a conclusion, which is why they posed the question, "When will this age end?"

The word "end" is the Greek word *sunteleias*, and it describes *the closure, the summation*, or *the wrap-up of the age*. Thus, the disciples were literally saying, "Lord, how will we know when this age is concluding and it's time for the next age to begin? How will we recognize that we've come to the very wrap-up of the age?"

Jesus Provided the Disciples With Many Signs

Just as most believers today are fascinated about knowing the future, so were the believers in the First Century. Jesus was very accommodating and gave His disciples not one sign but many authenticating signs that would categorically indicate when His return and the end of the age were near. The first and foremost marker He gave is found in Matthew 24:4 and 5:

> **And Jesus answered and said unto them, Take heed that no man deceive you. For many shall come in my name, saying, I am Christ; and shall deceive many.**

Worldwide deception — including deception in the Church — is a major sign that we've come to the very end of the age. We studied this in detail in Lesson 3.

Then in Matthew 24:6, Jesus pointed out two more major signs we'd see at the end of the age:

> **And ye shall hear of wars and rumours of wars: see that ye be not troubled: for all these things must come to pass, but the end is not yet.**

In Lesson 4, we noted that the word "rumors" in this verse is the Greek word *akoe*, and it describes *the human ear* or *something heard in the ear*, hence, *a rumor*. Essentially, Jesus said, "There will be the sound of war ringing in your ears." But because it's a "rumor" — something you hear and not something you see — He's really prophesying *the nonstop flow of information* at the end of the last days. Indeed, we are living in the information age, and the roar of the news is growing louder and louder. Our eyes and ears are going to be filled with rumors of conflicts all over the world. Nevertheless, Jesus doesn't want us to be terrorized internally by what we hear.

In addition to wars and rumors of wars, Jesus also predicted in Matthew 24:7 that…

> **…Nation shall rise against nation, and kingdom against kingdom….**

We saw that in the Greek, the word "nation" is the word *ethnos*, which describes *ethnic groups* or *religious groups*. And the word "kingdom" is the Greek word *basileia*, which describes *ideology* or even *a political realm*. Essentially, Jesus prophesied that at the end of the age, *ethnic groups* will rise against *ethnic groups*, *political groups* will rise up against *political groups*, and one *cultural ideology* will rise up against another *cultural ideology*.

The word "against," which appears twice in this verse, is the Greek word *epi*, and it carries the idea of *superiority* or *mastery over another*. It pictures *a crushing or subjugating force* that attempts to *decimate* its opponent in order to obtain the upper hand.

In Matthew 24:7, Jesus went on to say,

> **…And there shall be famines, and pestilences….**

We learned in Lesson 5 that the word "famines" in Greek describes *worldwide hunger* and *financial instability*, and the word "pestilences" is a medical term that refers to *old diseases that are revived and newly emerging diseases*. Jesus prophesied that famines and pestilences will be two more authenticating signs that we will see before His return and before the end of the age.

There was one more sign Jesus added in Matthew 24:7. He said those of us who are living in the last of the last days will see "…earthquakes, in divers places." Then after giving us all these signs, Jesus makes this very unique statement in Matthew 24:8:

All these are the beginning of sorrows.

The word "sorrows" here is the Greek word *oodin*, which describes *birth pains* or *the pain of childbirth*. It is the very word which denotes the *contractions* a woman experiences when she enters transition and is about to give birth to her child. Once those contractions start, they cannot be stopped.

By using this word "sorrows" — the Greek word *oodin* — Jesus is telling us that before His return and the wrap-up of this age, the world and its inhabitants will begin to experience contraction-like pains. The world is in transition to a new age, and these signs are leading up to the birth of it. The closer and closer we get to the very end, the greater the frequency and intensity of the pains society will be experiencing — it will be just like a woman getting ready to give birth to her child.

Before Christ's Return the Church Will Experience Persecution

In Matthew 24:9, Jesus began to prophesy about a time of persecution that would come to Christians in the last days. He said, "Then shall they deliver you up to be afflicted, and shall kill you: and ye shall be hated of all nations for my name's sake."

The word "afflicted" here is the Greek word *thlipsis*, which always describes *pressure*, *stress* or *stressful situations*. It depicts *tribulation, trouble, great pressure, crushing pressure, suffocating pressure*, or *a horribly tight, life-threatening squeeze*. We could say that *thlipsis* — this word "afflicted" — is a picture of one who feels trapped and unable to move. He has so much pressure upon him that he's barely able to breathe. An example would be the pressure from family and friends, hostile reactions from fellow workers, or the loss of employment due to one's faith.

In other words, *thlipsis* — this word "affliction" — depicts event piled on top of event to cause a weight so heavy that it feels nearly crushing. It depicts *bullying, harassment, and intimidation*. Early believers experienced these things, but Jesus used this word "afflicted" — the Greek word *thlipsis* — to depict a persecution that will arise again at the end of the age.

Next, notice the word "kill." It is translated from the Greek word *apokteino*, a horrible word that means *to massacre, butcher, ruthlessly kill, torture,* or *outright slaughter.* It can also denote *the giving of a death sentence.* We know from early history that believers suffered for their faith and were even killed, especially in the first three centuries. But it is happening again today in many parts of the world where Christians are being killed for their faith.

Jesus also said that believers would be "hated" for His name's sake as we approach the very end of the age. In Greek, the word "hated" is *miseo*, which means *to hate* or *abhor.* It describes *something utterly repulsive, a deep-seated animosity, intense hatred,* or *repugnance.* This word *miseo* — translated here as "hated" — can also denote *something objectionable* or *something that causes one to feel disgust and repulsion.* This is a *deep-seated aversion; not just a case of dislike.* It is a case of actual, undiluted hatred.

Many Will Be 'Offended'

Along with being hated, the overwhelming pressure of affliction, and the threat of death, Jesus said, "And then shall many be offended, and shall betray one another, and shall hate one another" (Matthew 24:10).

The word "offended" in this verse is a translation of the Greek word *skandalidzo*, which is where we get the word *scandal* or *to scandalize.* It describes *a scandalous situation that entraps someone.* In the First Century, the Christian faith was *scandalous* because believers lived by a solid, biblical foundation in a tossing sea of philosophy that held no moral absolutes — a cultural climate very similar to what is developing today. Christians at that time were viewed as bigots and narrow-minded simpletons just for standing true to their convictions and to their faith.

Worst of all, from the perspective of the pagan society that was around them, Christians were limited and narrow minded, largely because they believed Jesus was ***the*** way, ***the*** truth, and ***the*** life (*see* John 14:6). And because they trusted Jesus as the exclusive way to God, those who were around them said, "How dare you say that you're the only one who knows the right way!" Consequently, pressure was put on believers to modify their faith and become more inclusive, adaptable, and open-minded of those with differing spiritual views.

Offense Will Open the Door to 'Betrayal'

Jesus said the proliferating disease of offense will give way to people *betraying* one another. The word "betray" in Matthew 24:10 is the Greek word *paradidomi*, which means *to deliver or to hand something over to someone else*; *to betray by delivering* — usually to the authorities.

Luke elaborated on this epidemic of betrayal Jesus talked about. He quoted Jesus as saying, "And ye shall be betrayed both by parents, and brethren, and kinsfolks, and friends; and some of you shall they cause to be put to death. And ye shall be hated of all men for my name's sake" (Luke 21:16,17).

Although you may not have personally felt the brunt of this level of betrayal, there are many believers around the world today who are suffering in this way for their faith. They're being turned over to the local authorities and treated horribly. As society becomes more "progressive" in its thinking, biblical standards will be thrown to the wind more and more, and those who are uncommitted to the Word of God or who have toxic feelings toward it, may oppose and even ruthlessly stand against us who stand by the Book.

Again, along with betrayal, Jesus said Christians would be "…hated of all men for [His] name's sake" (Luke 21:17). The word "hated" here in Luke's gospel is the same word for "hated" in Matthew 24:9. It is the Greek word *miseo*, which means unbelievers will *have a deep-seated animosity and intense hatred* for Christians. Jesus predicted this would happen in various places and various times because of our faith in and devotion to Him.

Some Believers Will Be Entrapped, Arrested, and Imprisoned

What else did Jesus say would take place? He said, "…They shall lay their hands on you, and persecute you, delivering you up to the synagogues, and into prisons, being brought before kings and rulers for my name's sake" (Luke 21:12). When Jesus said, "They shall lay their hands on you," He was describing *physical arrest*.

Additionally, He said the world will "persecute" believers. In Greek, the word "persecute" is the hunting term *dioko*, which means *to hunt, to chase, or to pursue*; *to persecute*. It denotes the actions of a hunter who followed after an animal in order to apprehend, to capture, or to kill it. This word carries the idea of strategically following after an object, principle, or person until it is captured and caught. By using this word *dioko*, Jesus is telling us that unbelievers are going to set traps or devise schemes that will cause Christians to violate the law and be entrapped.

Once entrapped, Jesus said believers would be "delivered up to the synagogues." Now when you hear the word "synagogues," you probably think of a Jewish synagogue where Jews studied the Scriptures and worshiped God. Although this is true, local synagogues were also places where court judgments were issued by Jewish officials to those found guilty of a crime. Therefore, the word "synagogue" here corresponds with the idea of *a court system*.

After believers are pursued and entrapped (*dioko*), they will be arrested and handed over to the courts and placed into "prisons." The Greek word for "prisons" here is *phulake*, and it describes *a place of custody, a jail where one serves a sentence that has been rendered for his or her alleged offense*. This shows the power of government in the last days to inflict judgment on those who will not comply with new emerging societal standards.

At this present moment, 245 million Christians worldwide are suffering for their faith for various reasons. It is mainly because they refuse to bend to world trends. They are not inclusive or open-minded about sin or what the world dictates they need to accept. Instead, they're standing by the principles of God's Word, and because of their stance, they have been placed on a crash course with the world around them. They are being bullied, intimidated, and are under great pressure. And because of new laws that Christians simply cannot abide by, they're being entrapped as they stand by the Word of God and being arrested and brought into the court system. The more society continues to withdraw from the time-tested standards and principles of Scripture and grab hold of "progressive" thinking, the more persecution will take place.

What Should You Do?

First of all, you need to find and get into a good, Bible-embracing church where you can grow in Christ and receive support from like-minded Christians. Likewise, you need to be in the Bible yourself and begin to really know the Word, because the Word will strengthen you like nothing else, serving as an anchor for your soul. And by all means, you need to know and be filled with the power of the Holy Spirit. He is the same Spirit that empowered Jesus when He lived on earth and the same Spirit that empowered believers in the Early Church to be witnesses for Him (*see* Acts 1:8). You can also pray fervently for our brothers and sisters in need, and be mindful and willing to do whatever is possible to help them in their tribulations.

In our next lesson, we will examine the next sign Jesus gave to confirm His return and that the end of the age is near — which is the emergence of false prophets.

STUDY QUESTIONS

> Study to shew thyself approved unto God, a workman that needeth not to be ashamed, rightly dividing the word of truth.
> — 2 Timothy 2:15

1. Immediately after alerting us of the persecution we would experience for His Name's sake, Jesus gave us a powerful word of encouragement in Luke 21:14,15 (also Luke 12:11,12). What did He promise in this passage that is echoed in Matthew 10:19,20 and Mark 13:11? Why do you think Jesus repeated this promise so many times? How does it personally raise your spirits?

2. If you are being persecuted, what does Jesus specifically tell you to do in Matthew 10:23?

3. God is well aware that the topic of persecution is not pleasant. That is why He offers many words of encouragement to you and Christians everywhere. Take time to reflect on what He promised in Isaiah 41:10 and 43:1-3 along with Jesus' words in Matthew 10:28-31; Luke 12:22-32; and John 16:33. How do these promises encourage you to obediently press on in the faith, trusting Him to keep you in His care?

4. What recurring promises are echoed in Psalm 31:23 and 37:28; Proverbs 2:8; and Second Timothy 4:18? What is the Holy Spirit speaking to you through these verses?

PRACTICAL APPLICATION

> But be ye doers of the word, and not hearers only, deceiving your own selves.
> — James 1:22

1. In the First Century, Christians tenaciously held on to the belief that Jesus is *the* way, *the* truth, and *the* life (*see* John 14:6). How about you? Do you believe this foundational truth, or do you find yourself wavering in your faith? What external pressures are you experiencing to be more inclusive, adaptable, and open-minded of those with differing spiritual views? What has been your normal response to these pressures (affliction)?

2. Jesus prophesied that in the last of the last days, believers around the world will experience various types of persecution (*see* Matthew 24:9,10; Luke 21:12,16,17). Have you personally experienced any forms of persecution at the hands of family members, coworkers, or others? If so, briefly share what happened? How has this experience brought you closer to Jesus and strengthened your faith?

LESSON 8

TOPIC

The Emergence of False Prophets

SCRIPTURES

1. **Matthew 24:3-11** — And as he sat upon the mount of Olives, the disciples came unto him privately, saying, Tell us, when shall these things be? and what shall be the sign of thy coming, and of the end of the world? And Jesus answered and said unto them, Take heed that no man deceive you. For many shall come in my name, saying, I am Christ; and shall deceive many. And ye shall hear of wars and rumours of wars: see that ye be not troubled: for all these things must come to pass, but the end is not yet. For nation shall rise against nation, and kingdom against kingdom: and there shall be famines, and pestilences, and earthquakes, in divers places. All these are the beginning of sorrows. Then shall they deliver you up to be afflicted, and shall kill you: and ye shall be hated of all nations for my name's sake. And then shall many be offended, and shall betray one another, and shall hate one another. And many false prophets shall rise, and shall deceive many.

GREEK WORDS

1. "when" — ποτέ (*pote*): specific information; seeking a concrete answer
2. "what" — τι (*ti*): minute, minuscule detail; exactly; explicitly
3. "sign" — σημεῖον (*semeion*): a marker or sign to alert a traveler to where he is on a road; authenticating marks, or specific signs
4. "end" — συντέλειας (*sunteleias*): the closure, summation, or wrap-up of the age
5. "world" — αἰῶνος (*aionos*): not the world itself, but age
6. "false prophets" — ψευδοπροφήτης (*pseudoprophetes*): false revelators; cult leaders; cultic movements
7. "many" — πολλοὶ (*polloi*): many; multitudes

SYNOPSIS

The land of Israel is truly a remarkable place. From the Sea of Galilee and the city of Capernaum to the Mount of Olives and the city of Jerusalem, the rich history of Scripture is everywhere. Take Jerusalem, for example. It is where Jesus walked and talked — where He was put on trial and condemned to die. Just outside its gates He was crucified, buried, and raised from the dead!

So much prophecy surrounds this city — a portion of which is yet to be fulfilled. This includes Jesus' return to earth to rapture His Church. But what's going to happen between now and then? The Bible gives us many specific signs we will see the closer we get to Christ's coming and the wrap-up of the age. That is what we have been studying in this series.

But what if He doesn't come back very soon and things continue to spin out of control morally? What are we supposed to do? How are we supposed to live? What should be our response to the decadence and decay that's taking place in society all around us? How can we protect our kids, our grandkids, and ourselves from being deceived — especially by the emergence of false prophets?

The emphasis of this lesson:

A major sign that Christ's return and the consummation of the age are near is the rise of false prophets and false religious movements. Jesus declared that multitudes of false prophets would deceive multitudes

of people. We are seeing this take place through cult movements like Mormonism, Hinduism, and numerous eastern religions.

A Review of Five Important Words From Our Anchor Verse

In Matthew 24, Jesus was speaking to His disciples, telling them candidly about things to come in the last days. Verse 3 says, "And as he sat upon the mount of Olives, the disciples came unto him privately, saying, Tell us, when shall these things be? and what shall be the sign of thy coming, and of the end of the world?"

We've seen that the word "when" is the Greek word *pote*, and it describes *specific information* or *a concrete answer*. By using this word, the disciples were basically saying, "Lord, please don't be vague with us. Be *specific* and *concrete*. Tell us *exactly* when these things are going to happen?"

Next, the disciples asked Jesus "what" the sign of His coming would be. The word "what" here is a form of the Greek word *ti*, which describes *the most minute, minuscule detail*. The disciples' use of this word was the equivalent of them saying, "Lord, be *precise*. Tell us *exactly* and *explicitly* what the sign of Your coming will be."

In Greek, the word for "sign" in this verse is the word *semeion*, and it describes *a marker or sign to alert a traveler to where he is on a road*. The purpose of this *authenticating mark* was to tell a person where he was. Without the help of signs, he would not know where he was on his journey and how much farther he would need to go to reach his destination. By using this word *semeion*, the disciples were saying, "Lord, what will be the authenticating signs to tell us where we are on God's prophetic calendar? What signs should we look for to confirm we're getting closer to Your return and the end of the world?

The word "end" in Matthew 24:3 is the Greek word *sunteleias*, which describes *the closure, summation, or wrap-up of something*. And the word "world" is the Greek word *aionos*, which would better be translated as *an age*. Just as every age eventually ends and gives birth to another, our present age is going to wrap up, and when it does, it will give birth to the Great Tribulation. By using the words *sunteleias* and *aionos* — translated here as "end of the world" — the disciples were saying, "Lord, please tell us *explicitly*, *concretely*, and *precisely* when all these things will be, and what

70 | STUDY GUIDE

will be the authenticating signs we will see on the prophetic road to let us know where we are and how much farther we have to go until we arrive at the consummation of this present age?"

An Overview of Matthew 24:4-10

There are about 15 specific signs Jesus gave us in verses 4 through 10 of Matthew 24 to alert us that we are on our way to the wrap-up of the age and will soon see His return. See how many signs you can pick out as you carefully read through and review this passage:

> **Verse 4: And Jesus answered and said unto them, Take heed that no man deceive you.**
>
> **Verse 5: For many shall come in my name, saying, I am Christ; and shall deceive many.**
>
> **Verse 6: And ye shall hear of wars and rumours of wars: see that ye be not troubled: for all these things must come to pass, but the end is not yet.**
>
> **Verse 7: For nation shall rise against nation, and kingdom against kingdom: and there shall be famines, and pestilences, and earthquakes, in divers places.**
>
> **Verse 8: All these are the beginning of sorrows.**
>
> **Verse 9: Then shall they deliver you up to be afflicted, and shall kill you: and ye shall be hated of all nations for my name's sake.**
>
> **Verse 10: And then shall many be offended, and shall betray one another, and shall hate one another.**

So far, we have seen that Jesus prophesied: worldwide deception, wars, the threat of wars, terrorism, racial and religious conflict, uncivil politics, famine, hunger, scarcities, diseases, plagues, earthquakes, fearful sights, and signs in the heavens. And all these signs will take place before His return. In our last lesson, we learned that Jesus also forecasted worldwide persecution will come to the Church at the very end of the age. More than likely, there was a time in the past when you never believed you would be persecuted for your faith — but today you're living with a very real possibility of persecution. The reason for this change is because your faith and society are going in two very different directions, and society is demanding that you bend and adjust to their standards.

This is what Jesus was talking about in Matthew 24:10. He forecasted that there will be a time of bullying, harassment, and intimidation against those who are people of faith. To stay strong in these trying times, we have to remain anchored in God's Word, filled with the power of the Holy Spirit, and actively doing what God has called us to do — shining the light of His love and truth through the witness of our lives and the words of our lips.

The Emergence of False Prophets

In Matthew 24:11, Jesus went on to say, "And many false prophets shall rise, and shall deceive many." The word "many" in this verse is the Greek word *polloi*, which means *many* or *multitudes*. It appears twice, which tells us there will be *multitudes* of false prophets that will arise to deceive *multitudes* of people at the end of the age. And there is no lessening of the word *polloi* — there is no other interpretation for it. Christ was forecasting a deception that will affect huge numbers of people, and it will take place at the hands of "false prophets."

The words "false prophets" is a translation of the Greek word *pseudoprophetes*. It is a compound of two words: the word *pseudo* and the word *prophetes*. The word *pseudo* means *false*, and the word *prophetes* is the word for *prophet*. When these words are compounded to form the word *pseudoprophetes*, the new word refers to *a pseudo prophet, a false prophet*, or *one who claims revelation and divine inspiration but is not sent by God*. He or she asserts to speak by supernatural revelation, but in fact that person, Jesus said, is *pseudo* or false.

Basically, the words "false prophets" in Greek would better be translated *false revelators*. It depicts cult leaders and can even portray the idea of *false religious movements*. Again, it comes from the word *pseudo*, which describes *something that is false*, and the word *prophetes*, which is the Greek word for a *prophet*. A false prophet is a *bogus* prophet.

Rick shared how his first contact with a false religion came while attending college. Watching a group of young men with shaved heads, wearing orange robes and dancing across the campus chanting some kind of mantra was a real wakeup call for him. There were many false religions that seemed to proliferate among the students at his university. You may have had a similar experience. But today, a visit to the religion section of any major bookstore will reveal that false religions are big business — not just among young people, but among people of all ages. Jesus prophesied that false religions would proliferate at the end of the age, and that is precisely what has happened in our time. Millions of people in the world today are being deceived by *pseudo* religious movements.

Some of these false prophets are knowingly lying in order to create a religious following. However, there are other false prophets that really believe what they're saying because they did have some kind of a supernatural encounter. Nevertheless, while they're speaking as a result of some type of eerie spiritual experience, it is still a *pseudo*, or *false*, encounter because it did not find its origination in God, and what they're saying doesn't agree with Scripture. Jesus called these individuals *false revelators* and said that at the end of the age, there will be many of them that will deceive multitudes.

Examples of False Religious Movements

Looking once more at Matthew 24:11, Jesus said, "And many false prophets shall rise, and shall deceive many." Notice the word "rise." It speaks of a phenomenon when religion that is false will rise in the world in a notable way. Without question, false religions have multiplied rapidly in our times, each one presenting its own version of truth. This is exactly what Jesus declared — that many of these will appear on the scene at the very, very end of the age.

If you research the false religions that currently exist, you will find that the list is long. In fact, to deal at length with this subject adequately would require multiple lessons because there are so many false religions in the world today. The truth is, there are multitudes of individuals and religious organizations that claim to be divinely authorized and inspired, but they are *false*, in that they do not represent the truth of the Bible.

Some of them might even preach and adhere to partial biblical truth, but the core Bible doctrines of salvation through Christ alone, His death, and His resurrection and His present-day position in ministry are erroneous. They are misleading multitudes and multitudes of their followers. A short list of some of these false religions would include:

Baha'i
Buddhism
Scientology
Hinduism
Unitarianism
Islam
Universalism (and Unitarian Universalism)
Mormonism
Jehovah's Witnesses
Christian Science
Edgar Cayce's Association (mysticism)
Sun Myung Moon (Unification movement/"Moonies")
Eastern cults (Hare Krishna, etc.)
New Age religions

Each of these religious movements had an originator or a founder who claimed some special visitation from God. Whether by an angel or a dream or some other supernatural means, he or she received so-called revelations that either do not exist within the Bible or alter the meaning of the Bible.

A Closer Look at a Few of the Common Cults

The Mormons: The founder of the modern-day Mormon movement — also known as The Church of Jesus Christ of Latter-day Saints — is Joseph Smith. He claimed to have been visited by an angel who gave him additional revelations, which he wrote down and called the Book of Mormon. This so-called "other bible" does not agree with the teachings of the Holy Scriptures.

Jehovah's Witnesses: Charles Taze Russell created this pseudo-religion in the late 1800s, but the movement didn't officially take on the name of Jehovah's Witnesses until after Russell's death in 1931. Basically, Russell strongly believed and taught that man's works restored purity to Christianity. He also purported that Jesus was *not* Jehovah God, but merely the archangel, Michael, that took on human form.

Christian Science: Mary Baker Eddy is the woman who founded the Christian Science movement. She claimed to have received a revelation based on some of what she read in the Bible. She referred to God as "Father-Mother God" and alleged that "Divine Science" and the Holy Spirit are one in the same. Overall, her revelations do not agree with scriptural truth, especially concerning the divinity of Jesus Christ.

Edgar Cayce's Association: Edgar Cayce, who is often called the sleeping prophet, is the founder of an organization of mysticism. Supposedly, his psychic abilities began manifesting in his early childhood, and when he reached adulthood, he claimed to connect with a "universal consciousness," giving prophetic utterances and psychic readings from a sleeplike state. Although this does not agree with the Bible, millions of people follow Cayce's teachings.

Sun Myung Moon: Reverend Moon founded a religion that is called by his name and is also known as the Unification Church or the "Moonies." Basically, he claimed that Jesus Himself appeared to him and said, "I failed in My task because I died on the Cross. So I'm authorizing you to be the new prince of peace and to begin the new family of God in the earth." Moon also advocated that "man is incarnate God" and the Holy Spirit is a female Spirit that cleanses the sins of mankind. Based on these and other supernatural revelations from his alleged encounter with Jesus, Reverend Moon birthed a whole movement that is false.

Eastern Cults: Sometimes referred to as Eastern Mysticism, these cults encompass a number of religious movements, including Bahaism, Hare Krishna, Transcendental Meditation, Yoga, and Zen Buddhism. Generally speaking, eastern cults promote ideas like: "God is in the heart of everyone"; "man is fully divine"; and Jesus is considered to be one of many "Masters," supposedly sharing an equal position of divinity with people like Buddha. Essentially, this group of false religions claims that you are "to be still and know *you* yourself are God," and "self-realization is how one enters the kingdom of heaven." These teachings are in direct opposition of Scripture and are part of the broad path that leads to destruction Jesus talked about in Matthew 7:13.

New Age movement: This is a conglomeration of all kinds of religious and spiritual influences that are filled with thousands and thousands of revelators, psychics, and mediums who claim to have tapped into new streams of divine energy. It is a fact that millions of people have been led astray by some form of New Age deception.

Jesus clearly said that at the very end of the age, many false prophets shall rise and deceive many, and that is exactly what has taken place. Don't be shocked at the strange concoctions of partial truths and cult religions that exist in the world today. Just take it as a sign that we're bumping into the end of the age. Jesus didn't tell us this to scare us, but to prepare us so that we would not be taken off guard by the things we're going to see as we draw closer to His return.

Friend, this age has just about run its course. The rapture of the Church is fast approaching, and God wants us to be prepared — and to be a bridge to as many lost people as possible, helping them find salvation through faith in Jesus Christ. That is why it is imperative that you know your Bible. Knowing God's Word will anchor you in truth and keep you from being led astray by false religions and the deception that is running rampant.

In our next lesson, we will dissect Matthew 24:12 and discover what Jesus meant when he said, "…Because iniquity shall abound, the love of many shall wax cold."

STUDY QUESTIONS

Study to shew thyself approved unto God, a workman that needeth not to be ashamed, rightly dividing the word of truth.
— 2 Timothy 2:15

If we were to take all the religions of the world and put them in one group and then take Christianity and place it in a group by itself, we would see something remarkable:

1. **All World Religions Make Two Claims:**
   - They allege that Jesus Christ is not the Son of God and God Himself.
   - Man can somehow, someway work his way into right relationship with God/attain Heaven.

2. **Christianity Makes These Two Claims**:
   - Jesus Christ **is** the Son of God and God Himself (*see* John 17:1-3; Matthew 8:29; 14:33; and 26:63,64; Mark 1:1; 14:61,62; Romans 1:2-4).
   - Man *cannot* work his way into right relationship with God/attain Heaven. Therefore, God took on human form in the Man Christ Jesus and paid the price for our sins, restoring us into right relationship with Himself (*see* John 14:6; 1 Timothy 2:5; Ephesians 2:1-9; Romans 3:20; Galatians 2:16).

Look up these scriptures declaring these two foundational truths and commit them to memory.

PRACTICAL APPLICATION

> But be ye doers of the word, and not hearers only, deceiving your own selves.
> —James 1:22

1. Rick shared how his first contact with a false religion came while attending college. Can you remember your first encounter with false religion? Which religious movement was it? How did you respond to what you heard? How did you treat the people who shared the message?

2. What is your normal response when a pair of Jehovah's Witnesses or Mormons come knocking at your door? Are you angry and enraged? Do you turn off the TV and quietly wait until they leave?

3. Instead of getting frustrated and annoyed because false prophets are on your porch, why not turn the situation into an opportunity to share the real Gospel! What does the Bible specifically say in First Peter 3:15 you are to do? And in what attitude should you do it?

4. Have you ever encountered a "false prophet" — *one who claims revelation and divine inspiration but is not sent by God*? If so, briefly share what took place. What happened that caused you to come to your senses and realize they were a fake?

LESSON 9

TOPIC
The Love of Many Will Wax Cold

SCRIPTURES

1. **Matthew 24:3-13** — And as he sat upon the mount of Olives, the disciples came unto him privately, saying, Tell us, when shall these things be? and what shall be the sign of thy coming, and of the end of the world? And Jesus answered and said unto them, Take heed that no man deceive you. For many shall come in my name, saying, I am Christ; and shall deceive many. And ye shall hear of wars and rumours of wars: see that ye be not troubled: for all these things must come to pass, but the end is not yet. For nation shall rise against nation, and kingdom against kingdom: and there shall be famines, and pestilences, and earthquakes, in divers places. All these are the beginning of sorrows. They shall deliver you up to be afflicted, and shall kill you: and ye shall be hated of all nations for my name's sake. And then shall many be offended, and shall betray one another, and shall hate one another; and many false prophets shall rise, and shall deceive many. And because iniquity shall abound, the love of many shall wax cold. But he that shall endure unto the end, the same shall be saved.

2. **2 Thessalonians 2:3** — Let no man deceive you by any means: for that day shall not come, except there come a falling away first, and that man of sin be revealed, the son of perdition.

1. **Matthew 24:37** — But as the days of Noah were, so shall also the coming of the Son of man be.

GREEK WORDS

1. "when" — ποτέ (*pote*): specific information; seeking a concrete answer
2. "what" — τι (*ti*): minute, minuscule detail; exactly; explicitly
3. "sign" — σημεῖον (*semeion*): a marker or sign to alert a traveler to where he is on a road; authenticating marks, or specific signs
4. "end" — συντέλειας (*sunteleias*): the closure, summation, or wrap-up of the age
5. "world" — αἰῶνος (*aionos*): not the world itself, but age

6. "iniquity" — ἀνομία (*anomia*): lawlessness; without law; a lawless attitude
7. "abound" — πληθύνω (*plethuno*): to increase to maximum capacity
8. "love" — ἀγάπη (*agape*): God's love; the use of ἀγάπη (agape) could only mean the love of believers; indicates a waning of love toward God and toward fellow believers
9. "wax cold" — ψύχω (*psucho*): cold air; a breeze that cools or freezes
10. "wax cold" — ψύχω (*psucho*): to grow cold; to be chilled; progressively chilled by a poisonous wind
11. "endure" — ὑπομένω (*hupomeno*)— to remain in one's spot; to keep a position; to resolve to maintain territory gained; in a military sense, it pictures soldiers ordered to maintain their positions even in the face of opposition; to defiantly stick it out regardless of pressures mounted against it; staying power; hang-in-there power; the attitude that holds out, holds on, outlasts, perseveres, and hangs in there, never giving up, refusing to surrender to obstacles, and turning down every opportunity to quit; it pictures one who is under a heavy load but refuses to bend, break, or surrender because he is convinced that the territory, promise, or principle under assault rightfully belongs to him
12. "end" — τέλος (*telos*): the ultimate conclusion or climax of a thing
13. "saved" — σῴζω (*sodzo*): to heal, but conveys the idea of wholeness or salvation; wholeness in every part of life; a touch of salvation that brings delivering and healing power that results in wholeness; to deliver one's country from enemies; to protect, keep safe, to keep under protection
14. "falling away" — ἀποστασία (*apostasia*): a falling away or revolt; describes political revolt
15. "first" — πρῶτον (*proton*): first in order; in first-place; to begin with
16. "abound" — πληθύνω (*plethuno*): increase; flourish; overflow; to grow at maximum capacity

SYNOPSIS

The Bible is filled with prophecies — many that have been fulfilled and many that are in the process of being fulfilled. Jesus returning to earth to set up His millennial kingdom in the city of Jerusalem is one such prophecy. But before that can happen, He must return to rapture the Church. This event will give birth to the Great Tribulation in which the Antichrist will be unveiled and rise up to rule all the nations of the earth. Many of the prophetic events leading up to Christ's return are discussed by the apostle Paul in Second Timothy 3 as well as by Jesus Himself in Matthew 24.

The Bible says that as Jesus sat upon the Mount of Olives, He looked at all His followers — both then and now — and pointed a prophetic finger 2,000 years into the future and forecasted the signs we could expect to see at the very end of the age. One of the things He said was, "And because iniquity shall abound, the love of many shall wax cold. But he that shall endure unto the end, the same shall be saved" (Matthew 24:12,13).

Friend, we are the ones living in the last of the last days. The Holy Spirit has tagged us to represent Christ in these final hours — a time in which the world and society seem to be morally spinning out of control. With the timeless wisdom of God's Word and the supernatural empowerment of the Holy Spirit, you can learn to live your life ablaze and avoid experiencing the love of God growing cold in you.

The emphasis of this lesson:

Jesus said lawlessness will increase and flourish at the end of the age, and because of this lawless attitude, the love of believers for God and for one another will wax cold. To stay passionate in our love for Jesus, we stand by the truth of God's Word and stay close to the fires of the Spirit.

A Review of Our Anchor Verse

Matthew 24:3 says, "And as he [Jesus] sat upon the mount of Olives, the disciples came unto him privately, saying, Tell us, when shall these things be? and what shall be the sign of thy coming, and of the end of the world?" The five important words in this verse that we really need to understand are:

"**When**": The disciples asked, "*When* shall these things be?" The word "when" is the Greek word *pote*, and it describes *specific information* and pictures *one seeking a concrete answer*. Essentially, the disciples asked Jesus, "Tell us *specifically* and *concretely* when all these things You've said will take place."

"**What**": The disciples asked, "*What* shall be the sign of thy coming?" In Greek, the word "what" is the word *ti*, and it describes *a minute, minuscule* *detail*. The use of this word tells us the disciples were saying, "Lord, don't be vague. Tell us *exactly* and *explicitly* — down to the tiniest detail — what the sign of Your coming will be."

"Sign": In Greek, the word "sign" is the word *semeion*, which describes *a marker or sign to alert a traveler to where he is on a road*. "Signs" are *authenticating markers* letting one know how much further he has to go to reach his destination. The use of this word is the equivalent of the disciples saying, "Lord, tell us *explicitly* what *authenticating signs* we will see on the road to the end of the world. What *markers* will indicate that Your coming is imminent?"

"End": The word "end" is the Greek word *sunteleias*, and it describes *the closure, summation, or wrap-up of something*. The disciples understood that eventually every age would run its course and come to an end. Hence, they were asking, "Lord, when will the world as we know it wrap up and conclude?"

"World": The Greek word for "world" here is *aionos*, and rather than describe the world, the earth, or the universe, *aionos* describes *an age*. Every age has a concrete beginning and a concrete end. By choosing the word *aionos*, the disciples were asking Jesus to tell them *explicitly* and *exactly* what the sign would be that would confirm without a doubt that they had reached the very end of the *age*.

Jesus Answered His Disciples
Matthew 24:4-11

In the last eight lessons, we have carefully examined about sixteen specific signs Jesus gave us in Matthew 24:4-11 — along with four additional signs listed in Luke 21:9 and 11. According to these authenticating markers, we are indeed at the very wrap up of the age and will soon see His return. Let's begin in Matthew 24:4 and quickly move through to verse 11 — establishing each sign Jesus pointed to in this passage:

> **And Jesus answered and said unto them, Take heed that no man deceive you.**
>
> **For many shall come in my name, saying, I am Christ; and shall deceive many.**

Worldwide deception and deception in the Church are two signs we will see.

And ye shall hear of wars and rumours of wars: see that ye be not troubled: for all these things must come to pass, but the end is not yet.

Wars and rumors of wars are also signs we'll see.

For nation shall rise against nation, and kingdom against kingdom: and there shall be famines, and pestilences, and earthquakes, in divers places.

Warring political systems, clash of cultures, famines, economic instability, pestilences, unknown diseases, and great seismic activity are seven more signs we can expect to see.

All these are the beginning of sorrows.

Then shall they deliver you up to be afflicted, and shall kill you: and ye shall be hated of all nations for my name's sake.

And then shall many be offended, and shall betray one another, and shall hate one another.

Widespread persecution, the legal prosecution of Christians, and the imprisonment of believers are three additional signs we can expect to see.

And many false prophets shall rise, and shall deceive many.

The emergence of false prophets is another sign we will see.

The four additional signs recorded by Luke the historian in Luke 21:9 and 11 are: *commotions, terrorism, fearful sights,* and *signs from the heavens.*

Lawlessness Will Abound at the End of the Age

In Matthew 24:12, Jesus went on to say, "And because iniquity shall abound, the love of many shall wax cold." This verse describes a coldness coming to many in the Church, and the reason we know this depicts people in the Church is because of the word for "love" that is used here. It is the Greek word *agape*, and it describes *the unconditional, immeasurable love that only comes from God.* Those in the world who are not saved do not possess the *agape* love of God. Therefore, the "love" being described in this verse that is waxing cold could only depict the *agape* love of believers for God and for one another. Jesus said that at the very end of the age, this love in the Church would begin to diminish, and it will be primarily due to "iniquity."

The Greek word for "iniquity" is *anomia*, which is from the word *nomas*, the word for *law*. But when you attach an "*a*" to the front of the word, it cancels or reverses the meaning. Hence, *anomia* means *without law* or *lawless*. In this verse it actually describes *lawlessness*. A literal translation of this passage could be, "Because lawlessness will abound, the love of many will wax cold."

Anomia — the word *lawless* — is plural here, which tells us this *lawlessness* will escalate around the world at the end of the age. It depicts the actions of an individual, or a group of people, or even a nation. It can even denote an entire society or culture that has chosen to live apart from God's laws and principles. Though this person or a group previously followed biblical laws and principles, they elected to forge their own way of doing things that is not founded on the principles of God's Word. Thus, they are *lawless*, giving their own newly evolving principles to be their new foundation instead of living on truths that are portrayed in Scripture.

Jesus plainly stated that *lawlessness* (iniquity) will "abound" at the end of the age. In Greek, the word "abound" is the word *plethuno*, which means *to increase, flourish, and overflow; to increase to maximum capacity*. The use of this word tells us that this mass divergence or departure from the teaching of the Bible will escalate and proliferate at the end of the age and will reach maximum capacity. It is this *lawless attitude* that will cause the agape love of many believers in the Body of Christ to wax cold.

A 'Falling Away' Will Also Take Place

The apostle Paul refers to this worldwide rejection of biblical truth in Second Thessalonians 2:3. With a strong warning Paul wrote, "Let no man deceive you by any means: for that day shall not come, except there come a falling away first, and that man of sin be revealed, the son of perdition."

To be clear, when Paul says "that day," he is specifically referring to Jesus' sudden return to rapture the Church. Paul said that Jesus will not come until there is a "falling away first." The phrase "falling away" is a translation of the Greek word *apostasia*, which describes *a falling away* or *revolt*, or *a political revolt*. The word "first" is the Greek word *proton*, which means *first in order*, *in first-place*, or *to begin with*. Paul's choice to use this word *proton* emphatically means that before Jesus comes again, FIRST there is going to be *a revolt* or *mutiny against the authority of God and against biblical truth*.

This is what Paul prophetically described as a "falling away" that will transpire at the very end of the age. In that hour, the mystery of iniquity will be unleashed full steam in an attempt to lead the entire planet into various forms of deception. Once the Church has been caught up to meet the Lord in the air, which you can read about in First Thessalonians 4:17, the lost world will reject God all together and substitute Him with the "son of perdition," who is otherwise known as the *Antichrist*.

What is interesting is that the words "falling away" here are the very same words used in the Greek Old Testament Septuagint to depict *a mass mutiny against authority*. And by using this word, the apostle Paul, who was a brilliant linguist that knew exactly what the word meant, was saying, "Society will revolt against the authority of God Himself at the conclusion of the age."

Both Jesus and Paul prophesied a great "falling away" will occur in the last days. It will be a worldwide rebellion against God. In essence, Jesus said, "When you see lawlessness (iniquity) abounding — when you see a lawless attitude flourishing and increasing to maximum capacity — it will be a sure sign that you are colliding with the very end of the age."

The Love of Believers Will 'Wax Cold'

As lawlessness and a lack of moral understanding abound among the masses, society will continue to slide further and further into rebellion against God. In Matthew 24:12, Jesus was prophesying of a time that would come when immoral thinking, immoral believing, and immoral acting would affect nearly every facet of society. It will be a time of great moral confusion that leads to widespread immoral behaviors.

Looking once more at Matthew 24:12, Jesus said, "And because iniquity shall abound, the love of many shall wax cold." Again, the word for "love" here is the Greek word *agape*, which describes *God's love*. Thus, the use of the word *agape* could only indicate *the love of believers*. Here we see that there will be a *waning of love toward God and toward fellow believers*. It will "wax cold."

The words "wax cold" in Greek are a translation of the word *psucho*, which describes *cold air or a breeze that cools or freezes*. It can also mean *to grow cold*; *to be chilled*; or *to be progressively chilled by a poisonous wind*. Indeed, there is a wind blowing, and that wind is intended to chill the people of God in their faith.

This word *psucho* — translated here as "wax cold" — depicts people who progressively become coldhearted or who have become numbed. Perhaps they have become numbed by personal sin, by the condoning of sin, or by a sinful environment. Perhaps they have become cold spiritually by allowing the moral changes in the world around them to negatively affect their own standards. The lawlessness that abounds more and more may have rubbed off on them as well. Whatever the case may be, repentance is the key to getting back into right relationship with God.

Those Who 'Endure' to the End Will Be Saved

Immediately after warning us that the love of many believers will grow cold, Jesus said, "But he that shall endure unto the end, the same shall be saved" (Matthew 24:13). The word "endure" here is very important. It is the Greek word *hupomeno*, which means *to remain in one's spot* or *to keep a position*. It describes *a resolve to maintain territory gained*. In a military sense, it pictures soldiers ordered to maintain their positions even in the face of opposition. It means *to defiantly stick it out regardless of pressures mounted against it*. This word *hupomeno* — translated here as "endure" — is a picture of *staying power* or *hang-in-there power*. It is *the attitude that holds out, holds on, outlasts, perseveres, and hangs in there, never giving up, refusing to surrender to obstacles, and turning down every opportunity to quit*. It pictures *one who is under a heavy load but refuses to bend, break, or surrender because he is convinced that the territory, promise, or principle under assault rightfully belongs to him*.

If you want to experience the saving, preserving, delivering power of God, you have to stay put where He placed you. You have to stand by the teachings of the Bible and refuse to bend or back down from it. Regardless of what comes against you, you must choose not to surrender and turn down every opportunity to modify your faith in order to adapt to the world around you. That's what Jesus means when He said, "But he that shall *endure* unto the end, the same shall be saved" (Matthew 24:13).

The word "saved" here is the Greek word *sodzo*, which literally means *to heal*. In this case, it conveys the idea of *wholeness or salvation*; *wholeness in every part of life*. It is *a touch of salvation that brings delivering and healing power that results in wholeness*. It carries the idea of *delivering one's country from enemies*. It means *to protect, keep safe, to keep under protection*. In context here, Jesus is saying, "If you'll stick with the Bible, it will enable you to be preserved and protected all the way to the end."

God's Recipe for Remaining Red Hot

To maintain our fire for Jesus in these last days, we must choose to withdraw from ungodly influences that numb us and cause us to wax cold. It is essential that we stay close to the fires of the Spirit if we're going to stay passionate in our love for Jesus. If we make any other choice, we run the risk of allowing the lawlessness that is running amok in the world to affect us and to cause our love to go cold.

Friend, you do not want to wax cold in your love for Jesus or in your love for other believers. Jesus prophesied this will be a tendency for multitudes of Christians at the very end of the age. They will be infected by a lawless attitude that's going to proliferate in society. It is a wind blowing that is intended to chill the Church, luring believers to walk away from their firm commitment to the Bible and begin to be more open-minded and accepting of ungodly thinking and behavior.

You would be wise to keep your brain in your head and not be so open-minded that your brain falls out. God gave you a brain, and He gave you a Bible. You need to read it, believe it, and establish your life and your family on its principles. If you step away from the soundness of Scripture, you step toward growing cold in your passion for Jesus. Don't let that happen to you.

In our last lesson, we will focus on the ultimate sign that Jesus is coming soon.

STUDY QUESTIONS

Study to shew thyself approved unto God, a workman that needeth not to be ashamed, rightly dividing the word of truth.
— 2 Timothy 2:15

1. Before the antichrist is revealed and rises to power, Jesus will suddenly return to snatch up believers out of harm's way. According to First Thessalonians 4:15-17 and First Corinthians 15:51-53, what can you expect to take place at the time of the rapture of the Church?
2. Believers in all generations sometimes struggle to keep their love for Jesus burning brightly, and the Church of Ephesus is an example. What did Jesus say to these believers in Revelation 2:5 that they needed to do to rekindle the love they once had for Him? How can you personally apply Jesus' words in your own life?
3. What does the Bible have to say about staying on fire for God in these last days? Check out what the apostle Paul wrote in First Timothy 4:14 and Second Timothy 1:6. How do you think these instructions are connected with Jude 20; Ephesians 6:18; and First Corinthians 14:4?

PRACTICAL APPLICATION

> But be ye doers of the word, and not hearers only, deceiving your own selves.
> — James 1:22

1. Jesus said that *lawlessness* — choosing to live apart from God's laws and principles — will escalate around the world at the end of the age. In what ways are you seeing this happen in society or culture?
2. Be honest. With all the bizarre behavior and abandonment of biblical truth taking place, have you become spiritually *numb*? Has the *agape* love of God toward Him and toward other believers diminished in your life? Is it just the result of a sinful environment? Or is it a byproduct of personal sin or the condoning of sin? Ask the Holy Spirit to show you what is going on inside your heart. If you need to repent of sin and ask God to forgive you, take time to do that now.
3. To maintain your fire for Jesus in these last days, you must choose to tenaciously stand by the truth of God's Word and withdraw from ungodly influences that numb you and cause you to wax cold. Take a few moments to pray and say, *"Lord, are there any compromising or evil influences I need to pull away from? What can I adjust in my life to be able to spend more time in Your Word and in Your presence?"* Be still and listen. What is He showing you and asking you to do?

LESSON 10

TOPIC
The Ultimate Sign That Jesus Is Coming Soon

SCRIPTURES

1. **Matthew 24:3-14** — And as he sat upon the mount of Olives, the disciples came unto him privately, saying, Tell us, when shall these things be? and what shall be the sign of thy coming, and of the end of the world? And Jesus answered and said unto them, Take heed that no man deceive you. For many shall come in my name, saying, I am Christ; and shall deceive many. And ye shall hear of wars and rumours of wars: see that ye be not troubled: for all these things must come to pass, but the end is not yet. For nation shall rise against nation, and kingdom against kingdom: and there shall be famines, and pestilences, and earthquakes, in divers places. All these are the beginning of sorrows. They shall deliver you up to be afflicted, and shall kill you: and ye shall be hated of all nations for my name's sake. And then shall many be offended, and shall betray one another, and shall hate one another; and many false prophets shall rise, and shall deceive many. And because iniquity shall abound, the love of many shall wax cold. But he that shall endure unto the end, the same shall be saved. And this gospel of the kingdom shall be preached in all the world for a witness unto all nations; and then shall the end come.

2. **Daniel 12:4** — …many shall run to and fro, and knowledge shall be increased.

3. **2 Peter 3:9** — The Lord is not slack concerning His promise, as some count slackness; but is longsuffering to us-ward, not willing that any should perish, but that all should come to repentance.

GREEK WORDS

1. "when" — ποτέ (*pote*): specific information; seeking a concrete answer
2. "what" — τι (*ti*): minute, minuscule detail; exactly; explicitly

3. "sign" — σημεῖον (*semeion*): a marker or sign to alert a traveler to where he is on a road; authenticating marks, or specific signs
4. "end" — συντέλειας (*sunteleias*): the closure, summation, or wrap-up of the age
5. "world" — αἰῶνος (*aionos*): not the world itself, but age
6. "preached" — κηρύσσω (*kerusso*): preached; to be heralded by any means
7. "world" — οἰκουμένη (*oikoumene*): civilized, inhabited, sophisticated world; the technologically advanced world
8. "then" — τότε (*tote*): exactly then
9. "end" — τέλος (*telos*): the ultimate conclusion or climax of a thing
10. "nations" — ἔθνος (*ethnos*): nations; ethnic; ethnic groups; gentiles; it also expresses the idea of different customs, cultures, and civilizations; it pictures people from every culture, custom, civilization, race, color, or ethnicity in the world; all the various races and colors of human flesh; all the cultures of the world; all civilizations worldwide
11. "slack" — βραδύνω (*braduno*): tardy, slow, delayed, or late in time

SYNOPSIS

In Second Timothy 3, the apostle Paul describes in detail many of the things that are going to be taking place in society at the end of the age. Jesus Himself prophesied numerous signs that we would see as we get closer and closer to the end of the age and His return. What's interesting is that much of what they said is actually occurring right before our very eyes. Mindsets and behavior that were once considered so bizarre and outlandish have become commonplace.

Without question, we are living at the very end of the age, and since we are the ones that are going to see and experience all of these strange things, we need to know how to respond. Through the wisdom of God's Word and the empowerment and direction of the Holy Spirit, we can not only survive these times, but we can *thrive* in these times!

The emphasis of this lesson:

The ultimate sign that the very end of the age and Christ's return is near is the preaching and heralding of the Gospel to all who are living in the civilized, sophisticated world. The technological advancements of

our day have enabled this worldwide availability of the Gospel like no generation before.

A Final Review of Our Anchor Verse

After leaving the temple area in Jerusalem, Jesus and His disciples made their way to the Mount of Olives. And the Bible says, "And as he [Jesus] sat upon the mount of Olives, the disciples came unto him privately, saying, Tell us, when shall these things be? and what shall be the sign of thy coming, and of the end of the world?" (Matthew 24:3) Once more, let's look at the meaning of five key words in this verse.

The word **"when"** is the Greek word *pote*, and it describes *specific information* and pictures *one seeking a concrete answer*. The disciples asked for very specific, concrete information regarding when the things that Jesus had spoken of would take place.

The word **"what"** in Greek is the word *ti*, which describes *a minute, minuscule detail*. The use of this word lets us know that the disciples were saying, "Lord, don't be vague. Tell us *precisely*, down to the smallest detail, what the sign of Your coming will be."

The word **"sign"** in Greek is singular. It is the word *semeion*, and it describes *a marker or sign to alert a traveler to where he is on a road*. It was *an authenticating mark or specific sign* letting one know how much further he had to go to reach his destination. By using the word *semeion*, the disciples were saying, "Lord, tell us *explicitly* and *precisely* what signs we're going to see as we journey down the prophetic road to the end of the world. What will be the *signs* that tell us where we are prophetically and alert us to how much further we have to go before You return?"

The word **"world"** here is a poor translation. In Greek, it is the word *aionos*, which actually describes *an age*. The disciples understood that the current age would run its course and come to an end and give birth to another age. We know from Scripture that the next age will be the Great Tribulation.

The word **"end"** is the Greek word *sunteleias*, and it describes *the closure, summation, or wrap-up of something*. The inclusion of this word is the equivalent of the disciples saying, "Lord, tell us *exactly* and *specifically* when all these things will be. What will be the authenticating road markers to tell us where we are prophetically? And what will be the sign that this current age is about to wrap up?"

The Signs We'll See Before Jesus Comes

As we have noted, about one-third of the Bible deals with prophecy, and much of this centers on the return of Christ and the end of the age. Jesus' discussion with His disciples on the Mount of Olives is recorded in three of the four gospels — **Matthew 24:4-14; Mark 13:5-13;** and **Luke 21:8-19.** What are the signs that we will see on our way to the wrap up of the age?

1. Worldwide deception (Matthew 24:4)
2. Deception in the Church (Matthew 24:5)
3. Wars (Matthew 24:6)
4. Rumors of wars (Matthew 24:6)
5. Commotions (Luke 21:9)
6. Widespread terrorism (Luke 21:9)
7. Warring political systems (Matthew 24:7)
8. Clash of culture (Matthew 24:7)
9. Ethnic conflicts (Matthew 24:7)
10. Famines (Matthew 24:7)
11. Economic instability (Matthew 24:7)
12. Pestilences (Matthew 24:7)
13. Emergence of unknown diseases (Matthew 24:7)
14. Great seismic activity (Matthew 24:7)
15. Widespread persecution (Matthew 24:9)
16. Legal prosecution of Christians (Matthew 24:9)
17. Imprisonment of believers (Matthew 24:9)
18. Emergence of false prophets and false religious movements (Matthew 24:11)
19. Love of many waxing cold (Matthew 24:12)
20. Fearful sights (Luke 21:11)
21. Signs from the heaven s (Luke 21:11)
22. Worldwide preaching of the Gospel (Matthew 24:14)

All of these are signs that Jesus Himself said we would see as we come to the end of the age. The closer and closer we get to the end, the more frequent, the more numerous, and the more intense these signs will become.

Jesus Painted a Picture of the End of the Age For His Faithful Followers

Imagine you are on the Mount of Olives with the 12 disciples that day. The crowds are gone, and it is just you and His closest friends sitting with Jesus. This is not just a great Bible end-times teacher we are talking about — this is the Ancient of Days in the flesh explaining with flawless accuracy what you can expect to see before He returns and the present age wraps up. In that moment, Jesus turns to you and the Twelve and says,

> …Take heed that no man deceive you. For many shall come in my name, saying, I am Christ; and shall deceive many. And ye shall hear of wars and rumours of wars: see that ye be not troubled: for all these things must come to pass, but the end is not yet. For nation shall rise against nation, and kingdom against kingdom: and there shall be famines, and pestilences, and earthquakes, in divers places. All these are the beginning of sorrows.
>
> Then shall they deliver you up to be afflicted, and shall kill you: and ye shall be hated of all nations for my name's sake. And then shall many be offended, and shall betray one another, and shall hate one another. And many false prophets shall rise, and shall deceive many. And because iniquity shall abound, the love of many shall wax cold. But he that shall endure unto the end, the same shall be saved.
>
> Matthew 24:4-13

The Ultimate Sign of the End of the Age

Immediately after predicting all these signs, Jesus prophesied the ultimate, most glaring sign that would indicate that we have finally arrived at the end of the age. In Matthew 24:14 He declared, "And this gospel of the kingdom shall be preached in all the world for a witness unto all nations; and then shall the end come." To understand what Jesus is saying here, let's examine the original Greek meaning of a few key words.

First, notice the word **"preached."** It is the Greek word *kerusso*, which means *to preach* or *to be heralded by any means*.

Second is the word **"world."** In this case, it is not the word *aionos*, which means *age* and was used in Matthew 24:3. Nor is it the word *kosmos*, which denotes *organized society*, nor the word *gaze*, which is the term for the *earth*. Instead, it is the Greek word *oikoumene*, which is a compound of the words *oikas* and *mineo*. The word *oikas* is the Greek term for *a house*, and the word *mineo* means *to stay*. When these words are compounded to form the new word *oikoumene*, it describes *the civilized, inhabited, sophisticated world* or *the technologically advanced world*. It referred to the people who lived in the cities, towns, and villages of the civilized Roman world.

Next, notice the word **"then."** It is the Greek word *tote*, which means *exactly then* or *precisely then*.

This brings us to the word **"end,"** which is not the word *sunteleias* that we saw in Matthew 24:3. Rather, it is the Greek word *telos*, and it describes *the ultimate conclusion or climax of a thing*.

Putting the meanings of all these words together, we see that Jesus is saying, "When this gospel of the kingdom is preached and heralded to all who are living in the civilized, technologically advanced world as a witness unto all nations; then shall the end come."

In the Last Days, Knowledge Shall Increase

When Jesus gave the great commission to the apostles and to the Church (*see* Mathew 28:18-20), it was an enormous assignment. To preach the Gospel to the ends of their world meant they had to travel by ship, by mule, or on land by foot. It was very dangerous and very difficult. And because of the limitations of their time, they could not go into "all the world."

If you stop to think about it, it is quite remarkable how much of the world the disciples did actually go into and what they were able to accomplish given their limitations. They took the great commission very seriously, and to the best of their ability, they went into the world of their time.

In our lifetime, things are different due to our advanced technology. Today it is possible for us to reach the entire planet with the Gospel, which is actually a fulfillment of Daniel 12:4. In this verse, the Lord God spoke to

Daniel concerning the time of the end saying, "...Many shall run to and fro, and knowledge shall be increased.

Friend, we are living in that day. Knowledge has increased dramatically just in the last century. It is estimated that up until the year 1900, knowledge was doubling every 100 years. At the end of WWII, knowledge was doubling every 24 years. Today, researchers calculate with the continual expansion of the internet and advancements in technology that knowledge is doubling every 13 months.

Technology Has Made the Gospel Accessible Like Never Before

The fact is, most of the world can hear the Gospel today if they choose to hear it. For example, if someone has a mobile or smart phone, he or she has access to the preaching of the Gospel right in the palm of their hands. Likewise, if a person has a telephone, a radio, or access to the internet in some way, he has access to some form of the Gospel. Technology has truly changed everything, making it possible for nearly the whole world to hear the Gospel and in many cases, to even hear it in their own language.

Again, consider the original Greek meaning of what Jesus said in Matthew 24:14: "When this gospel of the kingdom is preached and heralded to all who are living in the civilized, technologically advanced world as a witness unto all nations; *then shall the end come.*"

Now we should note that the word "nations" in Matthew 24:14 is the Greek word *ethnos*, which is the same word we saw in verse 9. It means *nations* and describes *ethnic groups* — specifically the *gentiles*. It also expresses the idea of *different customs, cultures, and civilizations*. It pictures *people from every culture, custom, civilization, race, color, or ethnicity in the world*; *all the various races and colors of human flesh*; *all the cultures of the world*; *all civilizations worldwide.*

With all the advancements being made in technology today, we are not too far from being able to present the Gospel to every nation and every ethnic group in their own language. Probably the number one avenue through which the Gospel can be shared is the cell phone. It can access the internet and provides people with the ability to hear the message of Jesus — often in their own language.

Consider this: the population of the world today is nearly eight billion people, and of that eight billion, it is estimated that there are five billion mobile phones. Of course, not everyone with a phone is listening to the Gospel. Nevertheless, the fact is they have the technological means to access it and listen to it if they so choose. This worldwide availability of the Gospel has never happened before, and it could only occur at the very end of the age.

Christian programming, like Rick Renner's, is available to a large percentage of the population if they choose to watch it. In addition to the internet, there are also multiple TV and radio networks and channels that are carrying Christian broadcasting to many people in their own languages. Amazingly, we are living at a time when the Gospel is being preached and heralded to every ethnic group all across the civilized, sophisticated world. And Jesus said when this occurs, *then* the end will come. This means the end of the age — and Christ's return — are very, very near!

What Is Keeping Jesus From Coming Back?

Sometimes people say, "Why is it taking so long for Jesus to come back?" God answers this question clearly in Second Peter 3:9: "The Lord is not slack concerning His promise, as some men count slackness; but is longsuffering to us-ward, not willing that any should perish, but that all should come to repentance."

Notice it says God is not "slack" concerning His promise. The word "slack" is the Greek word *braduno*, which means He is *not tardy, slow, delayed, or late in time*. On the contrary, He is patient or longsuffering, not willing that anyone should perish. The truth is, God is waiting for the Gospel to reach the ends of the earth and for that last person He knows will respond to the Gospel and accept Jesus as his Lord and Savior to do so.

This life is racing toward the finish line, and everyone is going to spend eternity in either Heaven or hell. Unfortunately, many churches today don't teach about either place. They live as if there is no eternity and never offer people an invitation to receive Christ into their lives and repent of their sins. Their focus is on experiencing the best life they can, here and now. Nevertheless, God knows there is a literal hell, and He doesn't want anyone to go there because it is a place of eternal torture.

In His immeasurable mercy and compassion, God is requiring the Gospel to be preached and heralded by all means to all inhabitants of the civilized world before everything in this age is wrapped up. Jesus said in Matthew 24:14 that the preaching of the Gospel throughout the entire world will be the final indicator that we're living in the time just before He comes.

Friend, we're living in the age when more people have access to the preaching of the Gospel and the teaching of the Bible than ever before. It is the ultimate prophetic sign screaming at us that the wrap up of the age is almost here and Jesus is about to return for His Church. Our job is to preach and present the Gospel by any means to the whole world. Instead of drawing back from giving to missions, we need to continue supporting them with our finances and our prayers. There are people who still need to hear the Gospel.

Remember, Jesus told us the signs we would see before He comes are not to scare us but to prepare us to live victoriously in these last of the last days. May you be encouraged, empowered, and equipped to be actively engaged in reaching others with the Gospel and prepared for His soon return.

STUDY QUESTIONS

> **Study to shew thyself approved unto God, a workman that needeth not to be ashamed, rightly dividing the word of truth.**
> **— 2 Timothy 2:15**

It is very important for you to know God's heart with regards to people hearing the Gospel and spending eternity with Him in Heaven instead of being separated from Him forever in hell. Take a few moments to reflect on Second Peter 3:9 and on these passages:

- According to Ezekiel 18:23 and 33:11, how does God feel about punishing the wicked?
- According to Isaiah 1:18,19 and 55:1-3, what message is God speaking to those in rebellion?
- According to First Timothy 2:1-4, what does God want you to do that greatly pleases Him? Why?
- According to Titus 2:11-14, what did God promise is available to all men? Why is it given?

PRACTICAL APPLICATION

> But be ye doers of the word, and not hearers only,
> deceiving your own selves.
> —James 1:22

1. The apostles and believers in the Early Church took the great commission that Jesus gave — to go into all the world with the message of the Gospel — very seriously. Are you serious about sharing the Gospel with people in the world? In what ways are you actively involved in helping to spread the Good News of Jesus (i.e. in your prayers, financial giving, and participation)?

2. As the very end of the age rapidly approaches, the realization that this life is going to end and eternity is ahead and becoming very real. Jesus taught about eternity often, speaking about hell just as much — if not more — than He spoke about Heaven. As a Christian, why do you think it is important to never forget the reality of hell?

3. As you come to the end of these ten lessons on *Signs You'll See Just Before Jesus Comes*, what is one of the greatest takeaways from this study that you do not want to forget? Why is this important to you?

Notes

Notes

Notes

Notes

Notes

Notes

Notes

Notes

Notes

Notes

Notes

Notes

Notes

CPSIA information can be obtained
at www.ICGtesting.com
Printed in the USA
BVHW041828050521
606581BV00022B/386

9 781680 318630